FRANZ ZACH

DURCHST in Englisch

ENGLISH GRAMMAR

GRAMMATIK – TRAINING
Für die 5. – 8. Schulstufe

VER**I**TAS
LERNHILFEN

DURCHSTARTEN IN ENGLISH GRAMMAR, Grammatik-Training für die
5. bis 8. Schulstufe

Verfasser: Franz Zach

Diesem Buch ist ein Lösungsheft zu den Übungen beigelegt.
Das Buch ist nach der neuen Rechtschreibung abgefasst.

Bibliografische Information Der Deutschen Bibliothek
Die Deutsche Bibliothek verzeichnet diese Publikation in der Deutschen
Nationalbibliografie; detaillierte bibliografische Daten sind im Internet
über http://dnb.ddb.de abrufbar.

6. Auflage 2004

Gedruckt in Österreich auf umweltfreundlich hergestelltem Papier

Lektorat:	Klaus Kopinitsch
Herstellung, Layout:	Kurt Lackner
Illustrationen:	Bruno Haberzettl
Umschlaggestaltung:	Alexander Strohmaier
Satz:	Typomedia Grafik & Design, Neunkirchen
Druck, Bindung:	Landesverlag Druckservice, Linz

ISBN 3-7058-5308-2

Inhalt

Inhalt

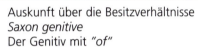

Inhalt

Inhalt

Welcome to English Grammar!

Mit diesem Buch hältst du die Fortsetzung und zugleich den Abschluss der erfolgreichen „Durchstarten in Englisch"-Reihe für die 5. und 8. Schulstufe in Händen. Sie bietet dir eine leicht verständliche und übersichtliche Zusammenstellung der wichtigsten Kapitel der englischen Sprachlehre. Das Buch enthält alles, was du nach vier Lernjahren wissen solltest, und noch ein bisschen mehr, damit du es auch später als Nachschlagewerk zum Auffrischen verwenden kannst. Diese Grammatik eignet sich somit als zuverlässiger Begleiter für alle, die gerade mit dem Erlernen der englischen Sprache beschäftigt sind, und ist zugleich ein ideales Mittel zur „Lückenbeseitigung" für Oberstufenschüler.

Der alphabetische Aufbau des Buches – von *„The Adjective"* bis *„Word Order"* – und die Seiteneinteilung – links die „Theorie", rechts die praktischen Übungsbeispiele aus der modernen Umgangssprache – erleichtern dir das Arbeiten mit dem Buch. „Schwierige" Punkte der englischen Grammatik werden ausführlicher erklärt und geübt, und dort, wo es notwendig erscheint, findest du Hinweise auf Verwechslungsgefahren und „Fallen" für deutschsprachige Lernende.

Wir hoffen, dass dir die bewährten Karikaturen von Bruno Haberzettl nicht nur die Zeit vertreiben und dich zum Lachen bringen, sondern dass sie dir auch helfen, einiges an „grauer Theorie" besser zu verstehen.

In diesem Sinn wünschen dir der Verfasser und der Verlag fröhliches und erfolgreiches Arbeiten mit dem Buch und viel Spaß beim Erlernen und Festigen der englischen Grammatik! Denke immer daran – so schwer kann Englisch nicht sein; immerhin wird es in Großbritannien, den USA und vielen anderen Ländern schon von den kleinen Kindern gesprochen!

1 The Adjective
Das Eigenschaftswort

Adjektive (Eigenschaftswörter) sagen uns, **wie etwas oder jemand ist.**
Sie beschreiben die **Eigenschaften** von Personen, Tieren und Dingen.

A Stellung des Adjektivs

1. Das Adjektiv steht

entweder **vor dem Nomen**, das es beschreibt:	oder **nach bestimmten Verben**, welche **Eigenschaften** oder **Zustände** beschreiben:
a **happy** smile	*Trudy **feels happy**.*
an **angry** man	*The man **got angry**.*
expensive clothes	*These clothes **are expensive**.*

2. Zur Gruppe der **„bestimmten Verben"** zählen:

- alle Formen von **to be**: *am – is – are; was – were; will be; …*
- die Verben **feel, look, smell, seem, sound** und **taste**
- die Verben **get** und **become** in der Bedeutung von „werden"

(Alle anderen Verben verlangen ein Adverb! Siehe Abschnitt **2D**, Seite 20.)

3. Diese Adjektive stehen **nie vor einem Nomen**:

- **ill** (krank) und **well** (gesund).

*The baby has been **ill** since Sunday. – Yes, he really doesn't look **well**.*

Daher nicht:		sondern:
~~an ill baby~~	→	a **sick** baby
~~a well baby~~	→	a **healthy** baby

Welche Adjektive gehören in welchen Satz? Wähle und setze ein!

> *great – great – true – tragic – famous – terrible – short – huge*
>
> *easy – young – hard – little – strict – happy – okay – great – good*
>
> *nice – friendly – beautiful – funny – little – good – talented – angry*
>
> *good – excellent – delicious – new – exotic – wonderful – favourite*
>
> *ill – sad – difficult – good – well – sick – right*

1. Benny is really very nice . He has a … smile, … blue eyes and … … dimples (= *Grübchen*) when he smiles. He is quite a … student and a … artist. He does not get … often, but when he does, it is better to stay away from him.

2. My dad is a very … baker. His cheesecakes are … and his applepies taste … , too. He likes to experiment with … recipes. Yesterday he baked an … fruitcake, with mangoes and pineapples. It smelled … ! I think it will become my … cake.

3. "Titanic" is a … film with … actors. It is based on a … story: the … sinking of the … ship in 1912. In that … catastrophe, more than 1,500 people lost their lives in a very … time. The ship sank 90 minutes after hitting a … iceberg.

4. I missed the maths test on Tuesday because I was … and could not go to school. But I was not very … about it because it seemed to be a … test and I'm not so … at maths. Now I have more time to prepare, but I am still not … The doctor said, "A … child should rest and not worry about school!", and I think he is …

5. It was not … to be … in the past. School was … work, there was … money and parents were very … I am … to live today. School is … , I have enough money and my parents are … (most of the time). I feel … !

The Adjective

Weitere Verwendungen des Adjektivs

1. Das Adjektiv kann auch **wie ein Nomen** verwendet werden.

Man meint dann eine ganze Gruppe.
the good and **the bad**   –   die Guten und die Bösen
"Give money for **the poor**!" –   „Spendet für die Armen!"

2. Auf die gleiche Art verwendet man auch Adjektive, welche die **Herkunft** (die Nationalität) anzeigen und auf **-ch**, **-sh** oder **-ese** enden.
the French, the Irish, the Portuguese –
die Franzosen, die Iren und die Portugiesen

3. Einige Adjektive stehen **im Plural** (Mehrzahl), wenn sie eine **ganze Gruppe** bezeichnen.
the blacks, the whites, the natives –
die Schwarzen, die Weißen, die Einheimischen

C

Adjektive in Verbindung mit *one* und *ones*

Das Adjektiv tritt oft gemeinsam mit dem Ersatzwort **one** oder **ones** auf. Das **Ersatzwort** steht dabei **anstelle eines Nomens**, das man nicht wiederholen will.
*The big car belongs to Harry, the **small one** is Fred's.*
*The white flowers are lilies, the **red ones** are roses.*

D

Reihenfolge bei mehreren Adjektiven

1. Wenn **mehr als ein Adjektiv** zur näheren Beschreibung einer Person, eines Tieres oder einer Sache verwendet wird, gilt die folgende Reihenfolge:

subjektiv vor objektiv – *"opinion before fact"*

a	**nice**	**young**	man
an	**ugly**	**modern**	building
some	**expensive**	**old wooden**	tables

2. Bei **mehreren „objektiven"** Adjektiven *("fact adjectives")* soll diese Abfolge eingehalten werden:

Größe	Alter	Farbe	Herkunft	Material	(Nomen)
a **big**	**old**		**Chinese**		**vase**
a	**new**	**yellow**		**plastic**	**tablecloth**
a **small**		**blue**	**English**		**car**

1B Setze die passenden Adjektive ein.

1. Polo is a sport for *(die Reichen)*.
2. *(die Alten)* often complain about modern times.
3. "The Black Rose" is the favourite bar of *(den Jungen)*.
4. What's *"(die Guten, die Bösen und die Hässlichen)"*? – It's the title of a western, but I don't know what it's called in German.
5. Both *(die Japaner)* and *(die Chinesen)* don't use our alphabet.
6. In the past *(die Franzosen)* and *(die Briten)* often fought each other.
7. If you lose your way, ask *(die Einheimischen)* for help.
8. For many years, *(die Schwarzen)* did not have the same rights as *(die Weißen)*.

1C Bilde Sätze mit *one / ones*. (Achte dabei auf die Steigerungsformen!)

> Beispiel: *small potatoes – bigger potatoes – cheap*
> The small potatoes are cheaper than the bigger **ones.**

1. cold milk – hot milk – tastes good
2. fresh strawberries – frozen strawberries – expensive
3. the red wine – the white wine – sweet
4. long skis – short skis – go fast
5. old people – young people – know much
6. your new glasses – your old glasses – look nice
7. the blue tickets – the yellow tickets – cheap
8. the white shirt – the pink shirt – small

1D Bringe die Adjektive in die richtige Reihenfolge.

1. brown eyes – *(tired, big)*
2. a black lady – *(old, friendly)*
3. a nice song – *(new, Italian)*
4. a new dress – *(red, wonderful)*
5. a black bag – *(big, leather)*
6. some French wines – *(old, good)*
7. old trousers – *(dirty, cotton, black)*
8. a blond girl – *(beautiful)*

The Adjective

Das Adjektiv macht Vergleiche möglich. Dafür braucht man die
Steigerungsstufen *(comparison of the adjective).*

positive Grundstufe	comparative Mehrstufe 1. Steigerungsstufe	superlative Meiststufe 2. Steigerungsstufe
wild expensive bad	wilder more expensive worse	wildest most expensive worst

Englische Adjektive bilden die Steigerung auf drei verschiedene Weisen.

1. Die **einfache Steigerung** mit **-(e)r** und **-(e)st** betrifft:

    einsilbige Adjektive → *strong – stronger – strongest*
                                      wide – wider – widest

    zweisilbige auf **-le,** → *simple – simpler – simplest*
    -er, -y und **-ow**   *clever – cleverer – cleverest*
                                        easy – easier – easiest
                                        narrow – narrower – narrowest

    zweisilbige, die auf der zweiten Silbe betont werden
                       → *polite – politer – politest*

Achtung auf die Rechtschreibung!

Einfacher Konsonant nach
einfachem Vokal wird **verdoppelt**:

hot   *hotter*   *hottest*

-y nach **Konsonant** wird zu **-i** :   *early   earlier   earliest*

2. Die **zusammengesetzte Steigerung** mit **more** und **most** betrifft:

    alle drei- und mehrsilbigen Adjektive
                → *difficult – **more** difficult – **most** difficult*
                   *unusual – **more** unusual – **most** unusual*

    alle anderen zweisilbigen
                → *famous – **more** famous – **most** famous*
                   *careless – **more** careless – **most** careless*

3. Die **unregelmäßige Steigerung** betrifft die folgenden Adjektive:

positive	comparative	superlative	deutsche Bedeutung
good	better	best	gut
bad	worse	worst	schlecht, böse
evil	worse	worst	böse, bösartig
well	better	best	gesund
ill	worse	worst	krank
many	more	most	viele
much	more	most	viel
little	less	least	wenig
little	smaller	smallest	klein
late	later	latest	spät (z.B. Uhrzeit)
	(the) latter	(the) last	letzterer – (der) letzte
near	nearer	nearest	nahe, nächst(gelegen)
		next	(der) Nächste in der Reihe
far	farther	farthest	weit (weg, entfernt)
	further	(furthest)	weitere (Fragen, Gäste, ...)
old	older	oldest	alt (normale Bedeutung)
	elder	eldest	älter, (der) älteste ...
			(nur bei Familienmitgliedern, nur vor dem Nomen)

1E Setze die richtigen Stufen der angegebenen Adjektive ein.

1. Did you see Joe yesterday? – Yes, he looked really *(ill)*. What's wrong with him? – I think he's got the flu. – I hope he'll get *(well)* soon. – So do I. There's nothing *(bad)* than lying in bed when the sun is shining.
2. Our school is a large building, but the new church is *(large)*. The train station is the *(large)* building in town, but it's much *(little)* than Victoria Station in London.
3. Today was the *(happy)* day in my life: Jenny said she loved me! She is really the *(lovely)* and *(wonderful)* girl in the world.
4. Which pizzeria is *(near)*, "da Antonio" or "Sorrento"? – The *(late)*, I think. It's just around the corner.
5. I love science, but Brigid, my *(old)* sister, hates it. – How *(old)* is she? – Sixteen. She's three years *(old)* than I.
6. You look tired! – Well, I had to walk all the way from the station, and it was *(far)* than I thought.
7. Have you read Stephen King's *(late)* book? – Yes, I think it's the *(good)* he has ever written. – Well, I think *"The Stand"* was even *(good)*.
8. In Amsterdam, they showed us the *(narrow)* house in town. It is only three metres *(wide)*.

The Adjective

F   Vergleiche

Vergleiche können verschieden aussehen.

Wenn man A mit B vergleicht, ist das leicht zu erkennen:
(a)   A ist **so** (groß, gut, ...) **wie** B – A ist **nicht so** (groß, gut, ...) **wie** B
(b)   A ist (größer, kleiner, ...) **als** B
(c)   A oder B ist **der-die-das** (größte, kleinste, ...)

Auf Englisch sieht das so aus:

(a) positive	(b) comparative	(c) superlative
as *(tall, good)* **as** **not so** *(tall, good)* **as** **not as** *(tall, good)* **as** *(tall, good)* **as** ...	*(taller, better)* **than** *(more, less)* **than**	**the** *(tallest, best)* **the** *(most, least)*

G   Zunehmende Steigerung

Daneben kennen wir die „zunehmende Steigerung" nach diesem Muster:
Der Wind wird <u>immer kälter</u>.
>   → *The wind is getting **colder and colder**.*

Die Schule wird <u>immer schwieriger</u>.
>   → *School is getting **more and more difficult**.*

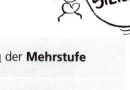

einfache Steigerung *(-er, -est)* unregelmäßige Steigerung	→ <u>Wiederholung</u> der **Mehrstufe**
zusammengesetzte Steigerung *(more, most)*	→ <u>Wiederholung</u> von ***more***

H   Vergleich mit „je – desto"

Der Vergleich mit **„je – desto"** verlangt den bestimmten Artikel *the* und die
Mehrstufe *(comparative)*.

<u>Je</u> billiger, <u>desto</u> besser. → *The **cheaper**, the **better**.*
<u>Je</u> länger wir warten, <u>desto</u> teurer wird alles.
>   → *The **longer** we wait, the **more expensive** everything gets.*

1F Denke logisch und bilde die richtigen Vergleiche.
The tiger is **stronger than** *most other animals in the jungle.*

1. You have to run *(fast)* ... you can if you want to catch your train.
2. We need your help, Gerry! Look at us, which of us is *(tall)* ..., Bill or I? – Bill is *(tall)* ... you. You are a little *(short)* ... he.
3. Some people think that dolphins are *(intelligent)* ... human beings. – I don't know, but they could be *(clever)*... animals.
4. What are your favourite clothes? – Jeans! I feel *(comfortable)* ... in them ... in anything else. And you? – Well, I like jeans, too, but I like dresses *(good)* ...
5. The accident with my bike was *(terrible)* ... experience of my life. It was much *(bad)* ... all my football injuries *(Verletzungen)* before and after.
6. Look at this man! *(tall)* ... a tree and *(strong)* ... an ox!
7. Which do you like *(good)* ..., history or geography? – Neither the one nor the other. I think one is *(boring)* ... the other.
8. You look happy, Fred. What's the matter? – Well, I bought this computer game, and it was *(expensive)* ... I thought. So I have some money left for a computer magazine.

1G Bilde die zunehmende Steigerung mit folgenden Beispielen.

1. The noise became *(loud)*.
2. The starship was moving *(fast)*.
3. I find physics and chemistry *(interesting)*.
4. I don't know what is the matter with me. I feel *(bad)*.
5. Many people feel that life is getting *(expensive)*.
6. The days are still warm, but the nights are getting *(cold)*.
7. Lola isn't my friend any more. I like her *(little)*.
8. My hairdresser wants *(much)* money for the same work.

1H Verändere die folgenden Sätze so, dass sich „je – desto"-Sätze ergeben.
If you drive fast, the risk of an accident is great.
The faster *you drive, the greater the risk of an accident.*

1. As people get older, they become wiser.
2. If the opponents *(Gegner)* are strong, the matches are exciting.
3. If I stay up late, I'm very fit in the morning.
4. If you study very long, you will remember very little.
5. If you worry a lot, you get wrinkles *(Falten)* in your face.
6. If you start soon, you'll get done early.
7. If you eat well, you will grow tall.
8. If we wait any longer, the situation will get serious.

The Adjective

2 The AdVerb
Das Umstandswort

Das Adverb (Umstandswort) **dient zur näheren Beschreibung** eines Verbs, eines Adjektivs oder eines anderen Adverbs. Es kann sich aber auch auf einen ganzen Satz beziehen.

Adverbs geben an:

wie etwas geschieht: → Art und Weise; *adverbs of manner*

wo und / oder **wann** etwas geschieht:
→ Ort und Zeit; *adverbs of place and time*
wie oft etwas geschieht:
→ Häufigkeit; *adverbs of frequency*

ob etwas **stärker oder schwächer** geschieht:
→ Grad, Ausmaß; *adverbs of degree*

wie ein ganzer Satz **gemeint** ist:
→ Satzadverb; *sentence adverbials*

A Bildung des Adverbs

Adverbs of manner werden im Regelfall nach der folgenden „Formel" gebildet:

$$adjective \ + \ ly$$

Dabei sind Rechtschreibregeln zu beachten!

Regelfälle					
adjective	→	adverb	adjective	→	adverb
sad		sad**ly**	basi*c*		basi**cally**
careful		careful**ly**	fantasti*c*		fantasti**cally**
			Achtung! Ausnahme!		
			publi*c*		publi**cly**

Achtung! Rechtschreibregeln beachten!					
adjective	→	adverb	adjective	→	adverb
easy		eas**ily**	terrib**le**		terrib**ly**
happy		happ**ily**	nob**le**		nob**ly**
Achtung! Ausnahme!					
shy		shy**ly**			

sadly, nicely, wonderfully, cheaply, ...
They <u>danced</u> **happily** around the new car. → how?

 here, there, everywhere, ...; today, tomorrow, ...
I <u>found</u> my skates **outside yesterday**. → where? when?

 always, frequently, hardly, never, often, sometimes, usually
(immer, häufig, kaum, nie, oft, manchmal, für gewöhnlich)
Grandma **sometimes** <u>visits</u> us at the weekend. → how often?

 fairly / quite / rather, really, very
(eher / ziemlich / recht, wirklich, sehr)
We have to get up **rather** <u>early</u>. → how (early)?

 actually, fortunately / luckily, frankly, unfortunately
(eigentlich, glücklicherweise, ehrlich, leider)
Actually, we didn't like the show very much.

2A Bilde aus den vorhandenen *adjectives* die entsprechenden *adverbs of manner*.

1. interesting – strong – great – sweet – wide
2. happy – wonderful – clever – narrow – polite
3. famous – bad – pretty – expensive – useful
4. economic – busy – dangerous – cheap – simple
5. dry – probable – sudden – public – thankful

The AdVerb

Unterschiedliche Bedeutung von Adjektiv und Adverb

Einige *adverbs* sehen so aus, als wären sie ganz „normal" durch das Anhängen von *-ly* an ein Adjektiv entstanden. Doch halt – der Schein trügt! **Adjektiv und Adverb** haben in diesen Fällen **unterschiedliche Bedeutung**.

adjectives		adverbs		examples
deep	tief	deeply	zutiefst	I have deep feelings for you. I am deeply in love with you.
direct	direkt	directly	gleich, sofort	This is a direct question. I'll answer it directly.
free	gratis	freely	freimütig, ohne Scheu	Free drinks for all! They ate and drank freely.
hard	hart, schwer	hardly	kaum	I am used to hard work. Bob hardly works for school.
high	hoch	highly	höchst, sehr	It's high time to go. He's highly respected.
late	spät	lately	vor kurzem, in letzter Zeit	Why are you late again? I've been busy lately.
most	am meisten	mostly	hauptsächlich	That's what I like most. It's mostly used by boys.
near	nahe	nearly	beinahe, fast	Mac lives near the park. He nearly had an accident.

Mad / hardly = kaum / fairly = ziemlich / pretty = ziem. / y - lin

Ausnahmen

1.

Einige *adverbs* werden **nicht durch Anhängen von *-ly*** gebildet. Entweder sie gleichen den entsprechenden Adjektiven oder sie sind „Sonderformen".

adj.	adverbs	Bedeutung	examples
good	well	gut	Mac and I are good friends. We get along well.
fast	fast	schnell, rasch	Mac likes fast cars. I think he drives too fast.
hard	hard	hart, schwer	For Mac, English is hard work. He has to work hard before a test.
high	high	hoch	Mac's house is on a high hill. The planes fly high above it.
early	early	früh, zeitig	Mac is an "early bird". He gets up early in the morning.
late	late	spät	Mac likes the late show on TV. So he is often late in the morning.

2.

Eine Reihe von Adjektiven auf *-ly* bilden **keine Adverben**. Man umschreibt mit *in a ... way*.

Zu dieser Gruppe gehören: ***friendly – lonely – lovely – silly***

2B Welche Form passt, *adjective* oder *adverb*? Überlege und streiche das falsche Wort durch.

1. Look, I've got *free / freely* tickets for the "Schürzenjäger" concert. Would you like to come along? – No, thanks. I *hard / hardly* know them. I think they are *most / mostly* for older people.
2. Be careful, you idiot! You *near / nearly* crashed into me! – Oh, I'm *deep / deeply* sorry! But if I don't hurry, I'll be *late / lately* again and this will land me in *deep / deeply* trouble.
3. Mt Palomar Observatory is on a *high / highly* hill *near / nearly* Los Angeles. Many *high / highly* respected astronomers work there.
4. What a *hard / hardly* test! I'll call you *direct / directly* when I get the results.
5. How are Mac and Judy? – I don't know. I haven't seen them *late / lately*. Have you? – No, I haven't. I *near / nearly* visited them last week, but then I didn't have the time.
6. Can I make a *direct / directly* phonecall from here to America? – Yes, you can. The first minute is *free / freely*, then it's 50 p per minute.
7. They said I could speak *free / freely*, but then they were *deep / deeply* disappointed when I said what I did not like.
8. That's what I hate *most / mostly*: *hard / hardly* work and *hard / hardly* any free time.

2C Suche passende *adjectives* und *adverbs* aus dem Rahmen und setze sie dort ein, wo sie hingehören.

> friendly – early – late – good – well – early – high – hard –
> good – fast – late – friendly – high – good – hard – fast

1. I know Martin ... He is a ... friend of my elder brother. They like mountains, and so they often leave ... in the morning to go climbing. They love to spend the day ... up in the rocks. Usually they return ... in the evening.
2. Martin is an ... riser. Even after a ... day of mountain climbing he does not sleep ... But he is always ... and has a ... word and smile for everybody.
3. He often thinks of the ... mountains that he loves so much. He is a ... and ... climber, but he is very careful, too. He practices ..., usually two hours every afternoon.
4. Martin is also a ... skier, but I think sometimes he skis too ... I hope I will be like Martin when I get older.

The Adverb

Verben, auf die kein Adverb folgt

Nach bestimmten Verben folgt das Adjektiv und nicht das Adverb. Diese Verben beschreiben **Zustände** und **nicht Handlungen** (siehe auch **1A**, Seite 8).

◆ alle Formen von **to be**:   You **are lucky** that I was there to help you.
         We **were happy** when we heard your voice.
         The holidays **will be wonderful**.
         The weather **has been terrible** this week.

◆ die Verben **feel, look, smell, seem, sound** und **taste** (wenn sie einen **Zustand** beschreiben):   I **feel awful** about this mistake.
         Jill **looked tired** yesterday, didn´t she?
         This **smells good**. What is it?
         This song **sounds great**. Who is singing?
         Your spaghetti always **taste** so **good**, Mary.

ABER: Jim **looked** <u>at me</u> **angrily**. = kein Zustand, sondern Handlung!
        The doctor **felt** <u>my arm</u> **carefully**. = kein Zustand, sondern ...
        I **tasted** <u>the spaghetti</u> **slowly**. = kein Zustand, ...

◆ die Verben **get, go, grow** und **become** in der Bedeutung von „werden":
        Stop this noise or I'll **go crazy**.
        Let's go inside. It's **getting cold**.
        Ben **grows impatient** easily.
        Sandra **became angry** when she saw me.

Steigerung des Adverbs

Auch das Adverb kann gesteigert werden *(comparison of the adverb)*.

Wie?	Was?	zum Beispiel:
-(e)r und **-(e)st**	alle *adverbs*, die **nicht** durch Anhängen von **-ly** an das *adjective* gebildet werden	*fast – faster – fastest* *hard – harder – hardest* *late – later – latest*
more und **most**	alle *adverbs*, die durch das **Anhängen von -ly** an das *adjective* gebildet werden	*careful – more carefully – most carefully* *slowly – more slowly – most slowly*
unregelmäßig	**well** **badly** **little** (wenig)	*well – better – best* *badly – worse – worst* *little – less – least*

             The Adverb

2D *Adjective or adverb?* Entscheide dich! Es gelten die Regeln 2B bis 2D, und auch die Steigerung der *adjectives* solltest du bedenken.

1. Do you know Julia Brown? – I think I do. Is she the *(beautiful)* girl who sings and dances so *(good)*? – Yes, that's her. She seems *(nice)*, doesn't she? – Yes, she does. But I don't know her very *(good)* I think you know her much *(good)* than I.
2. Why are you running around so *(nervous)*, Brian? – Well, I am *(real)* *(nervous)*. You see, Jenny has an *(important)* job interview today, and she said she would call me *(direct)* as soon as it was over. – Was Jenny *(excited)*, too, this morning? – Not *(real)*; she seemed very *(calm)* when she left the house. Of course, she had studied *(hard)* for this interview. She should *(easy)* get the job. I think she is the *(good)* for it!
3. Ah, this smells *(wonderful)*! What is it, Mom? – Apple pie. It is *(typical)* American. Would you like a piece? – Yes, please! Mmmmh, it tastes *(wonderful)*, too.
4. Do you like Mr Mulder? – No, I don't. I think he is a *(boring)* teacher. He often shouts at us *(angry)*, and we *(hard)* know why. Also, he speaks very *(dry)* and he never tells any jokes.
5. What's wrong with Mike? Why does he look so *(sad)*? – Haven't you heard? He had a *(bad)* accident last Thursday, and now his *(new)* racing bike is broken. – What happened? – Well, he was riding too *(fast)* and I think a little *(careless)*, too, when he crashed into a tree. *(lucky)*, he didn't break anything. – That's *(good)*! He was *(real)* *(lucky)*
6. What's this *(terrible)* smell? Has a stink bomb exploded somewhere? – No, that's the cheese Dad brought back from France. Don't you like it? You can say it *(free)*! – Like it? I think it's *(awful)* He should eat the thing *(quick)* and throw away the wrapping *(Verpackung)*. – I'm *(deep)* sorry that you don't like it. You see, it tastes *(excellent)*, too.

2E Verwandle die folgenden *adjectives* in *adverbs* und bilde die zwei Steigerungsstufen.

Beispiel: *happy* → *happily – more happily – most happily*

1. quick	4. early	7. slow	10. good
2. friendly	5. hard	8. polite	11. hungry
3. narrow	6. deep	9. fast	12. careful

Th**e AdV**e**r**b

Das **Adverb** hält sich an **die festen Regeln** der *word order*. (Siehe Kap. **25**, Seite 150.)

 F ## Zeit- und Ortsangaben

Adverbs of place und *adverbs of time* stehen entweder **am Beginn oder am Ende des Satzes**. Am Satzende steht „Ort vor Zeit".

> ***Tomorrow** Kim and I will talk to Mr Jackson about the school trip.*
> *We will talk to Mr Jackson about the school trip **tomorrow**.*
> ***Outside** it was much colder.*
> *It was much colder **outside**.*
> *Let´s play hide-and-seek **inside today**.*

 G ## Häufigkeitsadverben

Die Häufigkeitsadverben *(adverbs of frequency)* kommen in drei verschiedenen Positionen vor:

◆ **zwischen Subjekt und Prädikat** (das ist der „Normalfall"):
*Mum **often** invites her friends for tea on Fridays.*

S	adv	P

◆ **nach** der Form von *to be*:
*Willie was **never** the best at sports.*

	to be	adv

◆ **nach** dem ersten Prädikatsteil:
*I will **always** think of you.*

P1	adv	P2

 H ## Reihenfolge bei mehreren Adverben am Satzende

Das *adverb of manner* – das Adverb der Art und Weise (im Wesentlichen die Formen, die mit *-ly* gebildet werden) – steht in den **allermeisten Fällen am Satzende** (die Ausnahmefälle interessieren uns hier nicht). Wenn dort auch *adverbs of place* oder *adverbs of time* hinwollen, dann lautet die **Reihenfolge:**

manner	**place**	**time**
how?	where?	when?

*Sonya plays the piano **well**.*
　　　　　↓
　　　　　how?

*Buffalo Bill died **peacefully** in his bed.*
　　　　　↓　　　　　↓
　　　　　how?　　　where?

*Dad works **hard** at the office every day.*
　　　↓　　　↓　　　↓
　　　how?　where?　when?

The AdVerb

2F Setze die *adverbs* an die richtige Stelle. Bedenke, dass es manchmal auch mehr als eine richtige Möglichkeit gibt.

1. Peter practiced football. *(yesterday)*
2. Thomas Muster plays a match. *(today, here)*
3. Hermann will come to school again. *(tomorrow)*
4. Lots of people were waiting. *(everywhere)*
5. The children were playing. *(outside, yesterday)*
6. Thousands of people will watch the concert. *(here, tomorrow)*

2G Setze die *adverbs of frequency* an die passende Stelle. Achte dabei auf die verschiedenen Möglichkeiten.

1. Columbus set his foot on the American continent. *(never)*
2. I am interested in good films and books. *(always)*
3. Grandma has told me about her schooldays. *(often)*
4. You will remember her when you see her. *(hardly)*
5. The children were tired in the evening. *(usually)*
6. Dad drives to work. *(frequently)*
7. We make a barbeque in the garden. *(sometimes)*
8. You are writing with my pen! *(always)*

2H Setze die *adverbs* an die richtigen Stellen.

1. Mary smiled at me. *(happily, today)*
2. The visitors were waiting. *(outside, patiently)*
3. I'll have to work. *(tomorrow, hard)*
4. It rained. *(yesterday, heavily, here)*
5. Let's go! *(now, quickly, inside)*
6. Charlie sang. *(yesterday, beautifully)*

The AdVerb

3 The Article
Der Artikel

Im Englischen gibt es zwei Artikel:

1. den **unbestimmten Artikel**
(the indefinite article)
a oder *an*

2. den **bestimmten Artikel**
(the definite article)
the

Der unbestimmte Artikel *a / an* wird im Allgemeinen so verwendet wie auch im Deutschen. Dennoch gibt es ein paar **„Besonderheiten"**, auf die man achten muss!

 A   ## Aussprache

Der **unbestimmte Artikel** richtet sich nach der **Aussprache** des folgenden Wortes:

Wenn das folgende Wort **mit einem Vokal** (Selbstlaut) beginnt, heißt der unbestimmte Artikel *an*:

*an a*pple
*an h*our

Wenn das folgende Wort **mit einem Konsonant** (Mitlaut) beginnt, heißt der unbestimmte Artikel *a*:

*a w*indow
*a u*niform [juːnifɔːm]

 B   ## Bestimmte Angaben über eine Person

Der unbestimmte Artikel steht bei bestimmten **Angaben über eine Person** (Beruf, Herkunft, Religion):

My sister Karin is **a teacher**. – Meine Schwester ist Lehrerin.
Her husband Joe is **an American**. – ... Joe ist Amerikaner.
Joe is **a Protestant**, *but Karin is* **a Catholic** . – Joe ist Protestant, ...

 C   ## Wörter an nachgeordneter Stelle

Der unbestimmte Artikel folgt auf bestimmte Wörter an **nachgeordneter Stelle**. Merke dir die „verkehrte" Wortstellung!

half – quite / rather – such – what – once / twice

The beach was **half** *a mile from the hotel.* – ... eine halbe Meile ...
"Titanic" was **quite a / rather a** *good film.* – ... ein ziemlich guter Film.
Today is **such** *a nice day.* – ... so ein schöner Tag.
What *a strange story!* – Was für eine seltsame Geschichte!
Take these pills **twice** *a day.* – ... zweimal am Tag.

3A *a* oder *an*? Die Aussprache entscheidet!

1. This is ... easy exercise.
2. ... elephant is ... very clever animal.
3. "Jurassic Park" is ... exciting film. – Yes, and it's ... very interesting book, too.
4. I always take ... orange or ... banana to school with me.
5. Kevin has ... uncle and ... aunt in New York.
6. Volvo is ... European carmaker, Daewoo is ... Asian company.
7. Where have you been? The film was over ... hour ago.
8. Do you want to come to the cinema with us tomorrow? There's ... excellent film on. – I can't. I have ... appointment *(Termin)* with my dentist.

3B Erkennst du Beruf und Heimatland der folgenden Personen?

1. Mr Williams drives a school bus. He is ... bus driver.
2. Joe repairs cars.
3. Peter bakes bread, rolls and cakes.
4. Gillian makes or repairs dresses.
5. Martina takes pictures with her camera.
6. Mr Williams lives in Sydney.
7. Joe is from London.
8. Peter was born in Stuttgart.
9. Gillian lives in Toronto.
10. Martina is from Rome.

3C Wandle die folgenden Sätze so um (oder *"say it in English"*), dass ein unbestimmter Artikel an „nachgeordneter Stelle" steht.

1. This question is too difficult for me. – *(This is too difficult ...)*
2. For this cake you need 500 g of flour. *(→ ein halbes Kilo)*
3. Emily's party was quite nice. – *(That was ... at Emily's house.)*
4. Yesterday it was too hot to play outside.
5. That was a terrible mistake! *(Was für ein ...)*
6. Little Jake is now six months old. *(→ ein halbes Jahr)*
7. We were quite surprised to see Harry at the party. – *(It was ...)*
8. That's a very stupid idea, Bob!
9. The children made so much noise that I could not sleep.
10. This picture is beautiful! Did you paint it, Frank?
11. Ich habe zweimal pro Woche Klavierstunden. *(piano lessons)*
12. Meine Eltern gehen drei- oder viermal im (pro) Jahr in die Oper.

The Article

D Wendungen – *phrases* – mit unbestimmtem Artikel

Einige Wendungen – *phrases* – kommen ebenfalls nicht ohne den unbestimmten Artikel aus:

what a pity, it´s a pity	–	wie schade, es ist schade
(to have) ***a headache***	–	Kopfweh / Kopfschmerzen haben
(to be) ***in a hurry***	–	es eilig haben
in a moment	–	gleich, sofort
in a *(loud, low, shrill)* ***voice***	–	mit lauter, leiser, schriller Stimme

Der bestimmte Artikel **"the"** wird im Wesentlichen dann verwendet, wenn **bestimmte Dinge oder Personen** gemeint sind und nicht allgemeine. Der bestimmte Artikel kommt im Englischen **seltener vor** als im Deutschen.

allgemein → ohne *"the"*	**bestimmt → mit** *"the"*

E Herausheben einzelner Personen oder Dinge aus der allgemeinen Menge

***Children** like sweets.*
  (Kinder im Allgemeinen, alle Kinder)

*We gave **the children** some sweets.*
  (ganz bestimmte Kinder)

***Life** is full of surprises.*
  (das Leben an sich, ganz allgemein)

*I read a book about **the life of W. A. Mozart**.* (ein ganz bestimmtes Leben)

*Would you like **coke** or **milk**?*

*Is **the milk** fresh? – Is **the coke** cold?*

F Tage, Monate und Jahreszeiten

***Winter** is the best time of the year.*
  (Der Winter ist die ...)

The winter of 1997 was too cold.

*I hate **Monday** and **Tuesday** most.*
  (den Montag und den Dienstag)

*I first met Diana on **the Monday after Christmas**.*

*Both **March** and **May** have 31 days.*
  (sowohl der März als auch der Mai)

*Do you remember **the April of 1983**?*

The Article

3D   Setze die passenden *phrases* mit dem unbestimmten Artikel ein.

1. Terry spoke … *(leise)* so that we could
   hardly hear him.
2. The man was … *(hatte es eilig)* to leave
   before anyone could stop him.
3. "Lethal Weapon" is a great movie. … *(Es ist schade)*
   that you couldn't come and see it
   with us last night.
4. Juliet answered … *(mit lauter Stimme)*,
   "Yes, Romeo, I love you!"
5. Don't go away, I'll be with you … *(sofort)*.
6. … *(Wie schade)* that Ernie isn't here tonight
   He would enjoy this party very much.
7. … *(Es ist schade)* that you didn't see
   the beginning of the play.
8. Why are you … *(so eilig)*? Can't you take
   the next train?

3E   Welche Version stimmt? Denke daran: Kein bestimmter Artikel bei allgemeinen Fällen, sondern nur bei „bestimmten" Fällen!

1. *Butter* / *The butter* is made from *the milk* / *milk*.
2. I love *roses* / *the roses* in your garden.
3. How much did you pay for *the car* / *car*?
4. *People* / *the people* often don't know what to do in their sparetime.
5. My friends all like *music* / *the music*.
6. *Butter* / *the butter* is on *the kitchen table* / *kitchen table*.
7. I've always loved *the music* / *music* of the Rolling Stones.
8. Did you talk to *people* / *the people* over there?
9. Without *the electricity* / *electricity* *the life* / *life* would be very tough.
10. My favourite subject at school is *history* / *the history*.

3F   Wieder die Frage: Artikel – ja oder nein?

1. It often rains here in … autumn.
2. My friends and I usually go to the cinema on … Saturday.
3. … summer of 1998 was hot and dry.
4. School starts on … Monday after … first Sunday in …
   September.
5. … February is shorter than … January.
6. In … spring of 1938, German troops marched into Austria.
7. Thanksgiving Day is on … last Thursday in … November.
8. The next Olympic Games will be in … winter of 2002.
9. … August of 1983 was a special month: I was born then.
10. Schools are closed on … Tuesday after Easter.

The Article

G Vorsicht bei diesen Wörtern!

> school – university / college – hospital – church – prison
> bed – work

Most of the time **school** *is boring.* (das Lernen, der Unterricht)	*I went* **to the school** *to meet Linda.* (an den Ort, nicht als Schüler)
Gina is **in hospital** *after her fall.* (als Patientin, zur Behandlung)	*Tim is* **at the hospital** *to see Gina.* (als Besucher, nicht als Patient)
Joe came out of **prison** *yesterday.* (er „sitzt" nicht mehr, er ist frei)	*We met Joe* **in front of the prison**. (dort, vor dem Gebäude)
I often go **to church** *on Sunday.* (zum Beten, zum Gottesdienst)	*Let's go see* **the church** *and take some pictures.* (das Gebäude, nicht zum Beten)
Mike is **in bed** *because he's ill.* *You should go* **to bed** *now. It's late.*	*Mike slept in* **the bed** *that was used by Napoleon 200 years ago.*
After **work** *Dad often reads the paper.*	*I love* **the work** *that I am doing.*

H Vorsicht auch hier! Mahlzeiten – Materialien – Transportmittel

We serve **dinner** *from 7:30 to 10.*	*How was* **the dinner at "Sparro's"**?
Human beings need **air** *and* **water** *to survive.*	**The air that we breathe** *and* **the water that we drink** *must be clean.*
Many tourists arrive **by plane**.	**The plane from Paris** *is late again.*

I

Kein bestimmter Artikel bei:	Schon bestimmter Artikel bei:
Namen von Personen *(singular)* Ländernamen *(singular)* Berge Seen Straßen und Plätze vor *"most + noun"*	Namen von Personen *(plural)* Ländernamen *(plural)* Gebirge Flüsse und Meere —––- —––-

Joe Cooper *is my friend.* Jan and Rike are from **Holland**. I'd like to climb **Mt. Everest** one day. Bregenz is on **Lake Constance**. Our hotel is in **Fleet Street**. **Most people** like good music.	**The Coopers** *live on Main Street.* Holland is a part of **the Netherlands**. It is in **the Himalayas**. **The Rhine** flows into **the North Sea**. —––- —––-

The Article

3G Achtung! Der bestimmte Artikel verändert die Bedeutung eines Wortes!

1. Uncle Frank goes to ... church only at Christmas and at Easter.
2. I'm sorry but ... church is closed now. It opens again tomorrow.
3. The bus leaves from behind ... school at 12:30.
4. When do you get out of ... school today? – At a quarter to five.
5. Where's Doris? – She's waiting for us outside ... university.
6. When I'm older I'd like to go to ... college and study medicine.
7. In America, you go to ... prison for drunk driving.
8. Richard's father has a job at ... prison. He is a guard.
9. Doctor: "I have to send you to ... hospital."
10. Patient: "I want to go to ... hospital with the best doctors."
11. At what time do you usually go to ... bed? – At 9 or 9:30.
12. Is this ... bed your grandfather built for his first child?
13. I hope that all ... work we have done will be okay.
14. Dad usually takes the train to ... work.

3H Besonderer Fall oder allgemeiner Fall? Artikel oder kein Artikel?

1. _Lunch_ / _The lunch_ we had today was awful.
2. Our house is made of _wood_ / _the wood_.
3. This morning _the train_ / _train_ was late again.
4. Don't use _the wood_ / _wood_ of young trees!
5. Mum usually has a salad for _lunch_ / _the lunch_.
6. Dad usually goes to work _by train_ / _by the train_.
7. In England, _breakfast_ / _the breakfast_ is a big meal.
8. The Spaniards were looking for _the gold_ / _gold_ in South America.

3I _singular_ oder _plural_? Kein Artikel oder doch?

1. ... Canada and ... United States are English speaking countries.
2. The highest mountain in ... Sierra Nevada is ... Mount Whitney.
3. Sherlock Holmes's house was in ... Baker Street.
4. ... Niagara River connects ... Lake Erie and ... Lake Ontario.
5. ... Indian Ocean is larger than ... Atlantic and ... Pacific.
6. Where are ... Hendersons? – On holiday in ... Alps.
7. ... Nile, ... Amazon and ... Mississippi are mighty rivers.
8. ... most boys hate Barbie dolls, but ... girls love them.

The Article

4 Conditions
Bedingungssätze

if-sentences
conditions

Die Bedingungssätze – auf Englisch **conditional clauses** – kennst du auch als **„if-Sätze"**, weil sie mit dem Wort **if** (wenn, falls) eingeleitet werden.

Bei den Bedingungssätzen musst du Folgendes beachten:

- Eine Bedingung besteht immer aus **zwei Teilen**: dem **„wenn"-Teil** (eigentliche Bedingung; der „if-Satz") und dem **„dann"-Teil** (Folge, die eintritt, wenn die Bedingung erfüllt wird; der Hauptsatz).

Bedingung	→	Folge
If you ask me,	→	I will help you.

- Die **Reihenfolge** von „if-Satz" und Hauptsatz lässt sich **umdrehen**, ohne dass sich der Sinn des Ganzen verändert. Allerdings entfällt dann das Komma.

I will help you	→	if you ask me.

- Es gibt **drei Stufen** von Bedingungen (wirklich, möglich, unmöglich), die durch eine **ganz bestimmte Zeitenfolge** gekennzeichnet sind.

A „Fall der Wirklichkeit"

> Wenn die Bedingung **tatsächlich** (= wirklich) erfüllt wird, dann tritt die Folge **sicher** ein.

Diese Art von Bedingung verlangt:

present tense if-Satz	+	future tense Hauptsatz
If you **ask** me,	→	I **will help** you.
Wenn du mich (tatsächlich) bittest,		dann werde ich dir (wirklich) helfen.

4A Hier findest du verschiedene Übungsbeispiele zu den Punkten „Fall der Wirklichkeit" und „Bedingung und Folge".

Setze die Verben in Klammer in die richtige Zeitstufe (*present tense or future tense*).
Beispiel: *If the wind (get) stronger, we (not go) sailing.*
If the wind **gets** *stronger, we* **will not (won´t) go** *sailing.*

1. If I *(get)* a better mark next time, my parents *(buy)* me a new monitor.
2. If Mac *(not be)* at home, we *(go)* to the cinema without him.
3. If you *(not leave)* now, you *(not catch)* your train.
4. If Walter *(come)* to your party, I *(not speak)* with him.
5. Jack *(catch)* a cold if he *(go)* outside without a jacket.
6. Nothing *(happen)* if we *(not tell)* anybody about it.
7. Mr Jenkins *(be)* very angry if he *(find)* us in his garden again.
8. I *(not inform)* the police if you *(return)* my bike this afternoon.

Ergänze die folgenden Bedingungen mit den passenden Folgen. Achte dabei auf die richtige Zeitstufe.

people will never forgive us – we will watch another video film – I´ll give them to you – Grandpa will bring me his projector – if we don´t hurry – if you come after 5 – if Tom takes my bike again – if I can

9. If I find your glasses, ...
10. If it rains again tomorrow, ...
11. ... if he doesn´t forget it.
12. ... if we lose the next match.
13. ... he will be sorry.
14. ... we won´t be at home any more.
15. I will answer all your questions ...
16. Benny will leave without us ...

Conditions

B „Fall der Möglichkeit"

Wenn die Bedingung **vielleicht** (= <u>möglicherweise</u>) erfüllt wird, dann tritt die Folge **vielleicht** ein.

Diese Art von Bedingung verlangt:

past tense if-Satz	+	*conditional present / one* Hauptsatz
If you **asked** me,	→	I **would help** you.
Falls du mich (<u>möglicherweise</u>) bitten würdest,		dann würde ich dir (<u>vielleicht</u>) helfen.
		would + infinitive 1. Stammform

Bei **to be** gilt für <u>alle</u> Personen **"were"**, also auch bei *I, he, she, it*.
Allerdings hört man im modernen Alltagsenglisch immer öfter beide Formen:
 *If I **were** you, ...* und *If Joe **were** here, ...*
 If I <u>was</u> you, ... und *If Joe <u>was</u> here, ...*

Immer stärker wird **past tense** von **"would"** verdrängt, aber das hat sich noch nicht überall herumgesprochen. (Vergleiche: „würde"-Sätze auf Deutsch)
*If you **asked** me, I would help you.*
If you <u>would ask</u> me, I would help you.

C „Fall der Unmöglichkeit"

Die Bedingung kann nicht mehr erfüllt werden (= es ist **nicht mehr möglich**); daher tritt auch die Folge nicht mehr ein (= es ist **unmöglich**).

Diese Art von Bedingung verlangt:

past perfect tense if-Satz	+	*conditional perfect / two* Hauptsatz
If you **had asked** me,	→	I **would have helped** you.
Wenn du mich gefragt hättest (<u>hast du aber nicht</u>), ...		dann hätte ich dir geholfen (<u>konnte ich aber nicht</u>).
		would have + past participle 3. Stammform

4B

Übungsbeispiele zum „Fall der Möglichkeit".

Setze die Verben in Klammer in die richtigen Zeitstufen
(*past tense or conditional present*).

Beispiel: *If the wind (get) stronger,*
we (not go) sailing.
If the wind got *stronger,*
we would not go *sailing.*

if-Satz – Hauptsatz

past tense — conditional present

would + base form

1. If I *(get)* a better mark next time, my parents *(buy)* me a new monitor.
2. If Mac *(be)* at home, we *(go)* to the cinema together.
3. If you *(leave)* now, you *(not miss)* your train.
4. If Gina *(be)* a little friendlier, people *(like)* her better.
5. If Walter *(come)* to your party, I *(not speak)* with him.
6. Jack *(catch)* a cold if he *(go)* outside without a jacket.
7. Nobody *(notice)* anything if we *(not tell)* anybody about it.
8. Mr Jenkins *(be)* very angry if he *(find)* us in his garden again.
9. I *(not inform)* the police if you *(bring)* back my bike at once.
10. Charlie *(kiss)* Susi if he *(not be)* so shy.

4C

Übungsbeispiele zum „Fall der Unmöglichkeit".

Setze die Verben in Klammer in die richtigen Zeitstufen
(*past perfect tense or conditional perfect*).

Beispiel: *If the wind (get) stronger, we (not go) sailing.*
If the wind had got *stronger, we* would not have gone *sailing.*

1. If I *(get)* a better mark last time, my parents *(buy)* me a new monitor.
2. If Mac *(not be)* at home, we *(go)* to the cinema without him.
3. If you *(leave)* earlier, you *(not miss)* your train.
4. If Gina *(be)* a little friendlier, people *(like)* her better.
5. If Walter *(come)* to your party, I *(not speak)* with him.
6. Jack *(catch)* a cold if he *(go)* outside without a jacket.
7. Nobody *(notice)* anything if we *(keep)* quiet.
8. Mr Jenkins *(be)* very angry if he *(find)* us in his garden again.
9. I *(not inform)* the police if you *(bring)* back my bike at once.
10. Charlie *(kiss)* Susi if he *(not be)* so shy.

SEUFZ

Conditions

5 The Future
Die Zukunft

A **Bildung und Verwendung**

1. Die **Zukunft mit "will"** wird in allen Personen der Ein- und Mehrzahl auf die gleiche Weise gebildet:

	will (not) + base form (1. Stammform)		
I	will (not)	show	you my room tomorrow.
You	will (not)	see	my room tomorrow.
He / She / It	will (not)	be	very hungry soon.
We	will (not)	tell	anybody about it.
You	will (not)	find	your glasses here.
They	will (not)	come	here again.

• **Frage und Verneinung** werden „direkt" gebildet, also **ohne** Umschreibung mit **do / does**.
Will they come again? – They **will not / won´t** come again.

• Die **Kurzformen** verwendest du beim Sprechen und beim Schreiben von <u>persönlichen</u> Briefen und Dialogen, denn da sollst du ja so schreiben, „wie man spricht".

Dabei darfst du diese Formen und Wörter nicht miteinander verwechseln:

I´ll	= I will	≠	ill (krank)	**won´t**	= will not	≠	want (wollen)
we´ll	= we will	≠	well (gut)	**she´ll**	= she will	≠	shell (Muschel)

2. Die Zukunft mit **will** verwendest du bei **Annahmen, Erwartungen, Hoffnungen, Versprechen** und **Vorhersagen**, alles Ereignisse, über die du keine wirkliche Kontrolle hast. Häufig verwendete Wörter und Wendungen in diesem Zusammenhang: *probably, (I) expect, (I) hope, (I'm) sure* und *(I) think*.

I expect Mother **will like** the new earrings. (Annahme)
I think Joe **will do** the job very well. (Erwartung)
Let's hope the girls **will be** at the party, too. (Hoffnung)
I promise **I'll tidy up** my room this afternoon. (Versprechen)
It**'ll get** warmer soon. (Vorhersage)

3. Die Zunkunft mit *will* verwendest du auch bei (mehr oder weniger) **plötzlichen Entscheidungen**, oft mit *"I think ..."* oder *"I don´t think ..."*.

I'll go to the cinema with you. I have nothing else to do.
Have you asked your dad yet? – No, I forgot, but **I'll ask** him now.
I've got an English test tomorrow, but I don´t think **I'll study** tonight.

5A Alle Übungsbeispiele auf dieser Seite betreffen die Zukunft mit *"will"*.

Die einfachste Übung zuerst: Setze die folgenden Sätze in die Zukunft. Verwende dabei die vorgegebenen Zeitangaben (wo sie vorhanden sind) und bilde auch die Kurzformen.

Beispiel: *We <u>had</u> dinner at Trudy's house yesterday (some time).*
*We **will have (we´ll have)** dinner at Trudy's house some time.*

1. I <u>got</u> a new computer for my last *(next)* birthday.
2. In 1998 *(next year)* we <u>spent</u> our summer holidays in Portugal.
3. It <u>rained</u> yesterday. *(again tomorrow)*
4. I often <u>think</u> of you. *(always)*

Bilde alle Fragen (Entscheidungsfrage und die Fragen nach allen Satzteilen) und verneine den Satz.

5. Peter will buy Linda a bunch of flowers because he loves her.
6. The Prime Minister will open the new power station in Exeter next week.

Hier geht es um Annahmen, Erwartungen, Versprechen usw. Suche dir ein passendes Verb aus und vervollständige die Sätze.

notice – repair – have – be – probably want – land

7. In twenty years everbody ... computers with voice control.
8. Tell Fred about your moped. I´m sure he ... it for you.
9. If you tell Andy about the party, he ... to come, too.
10. What a silly mistake! I hope nobody ... it!
11. NASA say they ... on Mars some time around 2020.
12. Brenda hasn´t arrived yet. I expect she ... on the next train.

Jetzt sind rasche Entscheidungen gefragt! Suche dir wieder die passenden Verben aus!

never speak – go – have – call – stay – show

13. Are you hungry? – Yes, I am. I think I ... some bread and cheese.
14. I´m sorry, but Mr Wilson is out today. – Okay, so we ... again tomorrow.
15. I´d like to bake a cake, but there aren´t any eggs. – I ... and get some.
16. If you don´t stop telling lies about me, I ... with you again.
17. Can I see your new bike? – Not now, but I ... it to you tomorrow.
18. I don´t want to stay here all alone! – Okay, I ... with you if you like.

1. Die **Zukunft mit _"going to"_** wird mit den Präsensformen von **to be** (am, is, are) und dem Infinitiv (Nennform, 1. Stammform, base form) gebildet.

	to be	going to	base form	
I	am	going to	repair	my bike now.
You	are	going to	hear	a sad story.
He / She	is	going to	fall	asleep soon.
We	are	going to	take	a walk in a few minutes.
They	are	going to	start	the film now.

2. Du verwendest die _"going to"_–Zukunft **bei festen Absichten** oder **Vorhaben**.
We **are going to see** a film in the next biology class. (Der Lehrer hat es uns versprochen.)
I **am going to work** harder next time. (Ich habe es mir vorgenommen.)

3. Du kannst die Zukunft mit _"going to"_ auch verwenden, wenn **zukünftige Handlungen schon fest geplant** sind.
Allerdings zieht man im modernen Alltagsenglisch hier _present progressive_ vor (siehe auch Abschnitt **C**, Seite 38).
Don **is going to go** to a concert on Saturday. (Er hat schon die Karten.)
    → _Don is going to a concert on Saturday._
When **are** your parents **going to leave** for London?
    → _When are your parents leaving for London?_

4. Die Zukunft mit _"going to"_ heißt auch **nahe Zukunft** oder **near future**. Du verwendest sie immer dann, wenn du glaubst, dass etwas **sehr bald** – also in der „nahen Zukunft" – **geschehen wird**.
Meist weist irgendetwas in der Gegenwart auf dieses Geschehen hin.
Look, that man **is going to jump** from the high tower!
    (Er steht schon ganz vorne am Sprungbrett des Zehnmeterturmes.)
Take a warm coat with you. It´**s going to get** cold.
    (Die ersten Schneeflocken fallen schon.)

I'M GOING TO TAKE A REST NOW.

5. Du verwendest **was/were going to** für Handlungen, die in der **Vergangenheit geplant** waren („Ich wollte, …"), aber dann **nicht durchgeführt** wurden.
I **was going to wash** Dad´s car, but then Mike came and I forgot.
The girls **were going to be** at the dance, but they missed the bus.
**Weren´t** you **going to go** to the party? – Yes, but then I had a cold.

The Future

5B Die folgenden Übungen betreffen die **"going to"**-Zukunft.

Wir beginnen mit ganz leichten Umwandlungsaufgaben. Setze die folgenden Sätze in die Zukunft mit *going to*.

1. Sheila *(play)* the piano at the school concert next week.
2. I *(not listen)* to this silly talk any longer!
3. Helen and Sidney *(get)* married this summer.
4. Uncle Herbert *(open)* his own sandwich bar and I *(work)* for him.

Bei dieser Übung geht es um feste Vorhaben und Absichten. Suche dir ein passendes Verb aus und beantworte die folgenden Fragen sinnvoll (mit *"going to"*).

build – take – sell – not give up

5. What are the ambulance men doing in your house? – They ... grandma to hospital.
6. What'll your mother do with her old car? – She ... it.
7. What's John doing with all these boards? – He ... a tree house.
8. How was the French test, Gina? – Terrible, but I ...! Next time will be better, I'm sure.

In diesen Beispielen deutet alles darauf hin, dass (sehr bald) bestimmte Dinge geschehen werden. Suche dir pro Satz ein passendes Verb und bilde die *"near future"*.

make – be – rain – fall

9. Kevin has a difficult table tennis match tomorrow. It is 10 p.m. but he is still up. He ... very tired tomorrow morning.
10. This tree is dead. It ... over soon.
11. You don't know what you are doing. You ... me very angry!
12. It ... The sky is full of dark clouds.

Was war geplant, hat aber nicht geklappt?
Bilde Sätze mit *was / were going to.*

13. How did you get here so fast? – Well, I *(walk)* but then I decided to take the bus.
14. What a beautiful dress, Jane. Did you buy it yourself? – Yes. I *(buy)* a pair of trousers first, but then I saw this dress and I fell in love with it.
15. Does Jack still have his motorbike? – Yes. He *(sell)* it but he couldn't find anybody who wanted to buy it.
16. Did you and Bill play squash yesterday? – No. We *(meet)* in the afternoon, but then Bill called and said he was ill.

The Future

present progressive

Für **geplante Handlungen in der Zukunft** kannst du ***present progressive*** oder *"going to"* verwenden (siehe auch Abschnitt **B**, Seite 36).
Dabei darf die Zeitangabe nicht fehlen.
Present progressive wird allerdings häufiger verwendet als *"going to"*.

> Don **is going** to a concert on Saturday. (Er hat schon die Karten.)
> When **are** your parents **leaving** for London?
> (Welcher Tag steht auf dem Flugticket?)

Zur Erinnerung: ***present progressive*** bildest du mit

am		**present participle**
is	**+**	*(base form + ing)*
are		*("ing-form")*

present simple

In bestimmten Fällen verwendest du ***present simple* für zukünftige Ereignisse**. Dies gilt für Angaben im Zusammenhang mit Zeitplänen, Fahrplänen, Beginnzeiten und dergleichen.

> When **does** *"Men in Black"* **begin**? – At 8:30, I think.
> Uncle Conrad's plane **arrives** at 5:15.
> My first two lessons tomorrow **are** English and chemistry.

future progressive

Eine „typisch englische" Form der Zukunft ist ***future progressive***. Damit beschreibst du, was <u>zu einem zukünftigen Zeitpunkt</u> gerade im Gang sein wird. Du bildest *future progressive* in allen Personen der Ein- und Mehrzahl gleich:

> **will be + "ing-form"**

> <u>This time next week</u> I **will be studying** for my last exam,
> Michelle **will be making** her canoe trip and
> my parents **will be getting** ready for their holiday.

future perfect tense

Die **Vorzukunft** oder ***future perfect tense*** drückt aus, was <u>zu einer bestimmten Zeit in der Zukunft</u> schon geschehen sein wird. Du bildest *future perfect tense* in allen Personen der Ein- und Mehrzahl gleich:

> **will have + 3rd form**

> <u>This time next month</u> I **will have taken** my final exam,
> Michelle **will have returned** from Sweden and
> my parents **will have left** for France.

5C Hier findest du Roberts „Wochenplan" für die kommenden sieben Tage. Was hat er vor? Bilde Sätze mit *present progressive* (und mit *"going to"*).

Monday	6 p.m.	play squash with Jenny
Tuesday	third lesson	give talk about Hercules in history class
Thursday	1 p.m.	have lunch with parents in town
Friday	7 p.m.	take part in school concert

5D „Offizieller Zeitplan" oder „persönliche Planung"? *Present simple* oder *present progressive*?

1. We (meet) Aunt Elizabeth at the airport. Her plane (arrive) at 10:30.
2. The film (begin) at 7. I (go) with Alex, Verena and Lisa.
3. When (start) the Formula One race on TV? – At 2 p.m., but I (not watch) today. – Why not? – We (have) guests in the evening and I (help) my mother with the cooking.
4. Have you heard? Rita (come) home tomorrow. – Great! She (travel) by train or by car? – By train. It (leave) Rome at 6 p.m. today and (arrive) here at 10 a.m. tomorrow morning. – Who (meet) her at the station? – We are. We (leave) here at 8:30. Do you want to come with us? – No, I can't. I (play) a tennis tournament tomorrow.

5E + **5F** Setze die gegebenen Verben in *future progressive* und in *future perfect*.

1. On the spot where you are standing now they (build) a large swimming pool next spring.
2. This time next Friday we (visit) our friends in Switzerland.
3. This evening Uncle Walter (read) our letter.
4. On December 26, they (open) our presents.

Und jetzt alle Möglichkeiten der Zukunft gemeinsam!

1. Tom and Jerry (have) a party next Friday. Would you like to come? – We can't! We (go) to a concert. Mike has already got the tickets.
2. This time next week, hundreds of people (come) to ski here.
3. Dad's train (leave) in an hour. He (travel) to Berlin on business. His boss (come) with him. They (stay) until Friday.
4. Have you done your homework, Jacob? – No, not yet. I (do) it in the afternoon. – You can't do it in the afternoon. The Millers (come)!
5. Daniel, you've left the door open again! – I'm sorry. I (shut) it at once.
6. It (rain) tonight! I can feel it in my toes! – You and your toes! There are no clouds in the sky! I don't think there (be) any rain.
7. Last year, we (visit) Disney World, but then Mum was ill and we couldn't go. But this summer we (go). We already have the tickets to Florida. Our plane (leave) on July 6, at 8 o'clock in the morning.

The Future

6 Ţhe Gerund

Das **Gerund ist ein Verb, das wie ein Nomen verwendet** wird – ein „hauptwörtlich gebrauchtes Zeitwort". Überall dort, wo ein *gerund* steht, kann auch ein „normales" Nomen stehen.

Das Gerund ist eine **"ing-form"**. Die *"ing-form"* wird aus der 1. Stammform (*base form*) des Verbs durch Anhängen der Silbe „*-ing*" abgeleitet.

work + ing → working   play + ing → playing

Bei der Ableitung musst du **drei Rechtschreibregeln** beachten:

◆ Wegfall des „stummen e" am Ende der *base form*:
write → writing   come → coming

◆ Verdoppelung des Endkonsonanten bei kurzen *base forms*:
sit → sitting   stop → stopping

◆ *ie* zu *y* bei drei Verben:
lie → *lying*   *die* → *dying*   *tie* → *tying*
(liegen, lügen)   (sterben)   (binden, knüpfen)

A   Verwendung des Gerund

1.   Das **Gerund** kann **als Subjekt** und **als Objekt** auftreten, wie jedes andere Nomen auch. Dabei kann es von einem Artikel begleitet werden – oder nicht. (Du erfährst alles Wissenswerte über den Artikel in Kapitel **3**, ab Seite 24.)

Snowboarding is great fun.   (Snowboarden macht Spaß.)
The howling of the wind was terrible.   (Das Heulen des Windes ...)

George likes **dancing** with Bianca.
From our hotel we could hear **the crashing** of the waves.

2.   Das Gerund als Objekt tritt oft in Verbindung mit Verben auf, die **Vorliebe** oder **Abneigung** ausdrücken. Dazu zählen vor allem:

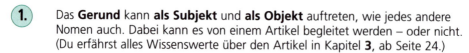

like – love – enjoy – dislike – hate

We <u>hate</u> **playing** football in the rain.
I really <u>enjoyed</u> **talking** to you.
Norman <u>loves</u> **cooking** for his guests.

Eine kleine Übung zum Aufwärmen und Wiederholen: Bilde die *"ing-forms"* der folgenden Verben. Beachte dabei die Rechtschreibregeln!

> ask – bring – cry – die – edit – fish – get – hide – joke
> inherit* – keep – lie – make – nag** – open – put – queue***
> question° – race – say – talk – use – vary°° – write – yell°°°

* erben	** nörgeln	*** sich anstellen
° befragen	°° sich unterscheiden	°°° schreien

6A

Das Gerund ist eine „typisch englische" Sache. Manchmal entspricht es seinem deutschen Gegenstück, oft aber unterscheidet es sich deutlich davon.
Du erkennst den Unterschied zwischen den zwei Sprachen am besten, wenn du den englischen Satz direkt mit dem deutschen vergleichst – mit Hilfe einer Übersetzungsübung!

Versuche, die englischen Sätze in „gutes" Deutsch zu übertragen! Wo wird im Deutschen aus dem Gerund ein Nomen, wo musst du zu einer anderen Lösung greifen?

1. I hate waiting for you every day.
2. My favourite hobby is collecting stamps.
3. The barking of the dogs made sleeping impossible.
4. Smoking and drinking are expensive and dangerous habits.
5. The thieves were driven away by the ringing of the alarm bell.
6. The chirping of the birds wakes me up every morning.
7. My sister likes knitting *(stricken)* pullovers for her friends.
8. Fishing in the sea is illegal.

The Gerund

Gerund nach Fügungen mit *"to be"*

Das Gerund ist **zwingend nach bestimmten Fügungen mit *"to be"***.

Das sieht dann zum Beispiel so aus:
> Martha *is proud of* **finishing** the race first.
> We *are far from* **speaking** English perfectly.

Die wichtigsten dieser Fügungen – aber bei weitem nicht alle – sind diese:

to be afraid of	sich fürchten vor, Angst haben vor	**to be proud of**	stolz sein auf
to be (in)capable of	(un)fähig sein zu etwas	**to be responsible for**	verantwortlich sein für
to be far from	weit entfernt sein von	**to be surprised at**	überrascht sein von / über
to be fond of	gerne tun oder haben	**to be tired of**	etwas satt haben
to be good at	gut sein bei / in	**to be tired from**	müde sein von
to be interested in	sich interessieren für, int. sein an	**to be used to**	gewöhnt sein an

Gerund nach „bestimmten Verben"

Das Gerund ist auch **zwingend nach bestimmten Verben**:

Das sieht dann zum Beispiel so aus:
> Can you *imagine* **owning** a million dollars and **living** in Hawaii?
> The kids *finished* **playing** and went home.

Die wichtigsten dieser Verben – aber bei weitem nicht alle – sind diese:

to admit	zugeben, gestehen	**to mind**	(etw.) dagegen haben
to avoid	vermeiden	**to miss**	(ver)missen
to begin	beginnen, anfangen	**to practice**	üben
to consider	überlegen, bedenken	**to risk**	riskieren
to finish	beenden, fertig werden	**to start**	beginnen, anfangen
to imagine	sich (etwas) vorstellen	**to stop**	aufhören
to mention	erwähnen	**to suggest**	vorschlagen

T̨he Geꭈund

6B Für die Fügungen mit *"to be"* eignen sich Übersetzungen wieder besonders gut. Bilde mit den angegebenen Verben *gerunds* und übersetze die englischen Sätze, die du so erhältst, ins Deutsche. Danach versuche, die deutschen Sätze ins Englische zu übertragen.

1. We are not afraid of *(fight)* with older boys.
   Als Kind hatte ich Angst davor, allein zu Hause zu sein.
2. I really don´t think that Janet is capable of *(lie)*.
   David war so müde, dass er unfähig war, das Rennen zu beenden.
3. Our new neighbours are very fond of *(have)* guests for dinner.
   Ich unterhalte mich gerne mit dir.
4. I´m not as good at *(play)* the piano as five years ago.
   Claudia ist sehr gut im Erfinden von Ausreden.
5. Are you interested in *(find)* out who really broke the window?
   Wir interessieren uns sehr für Reisen in ferne Länder.
6. Who is responsible for *(organize)* the school ball?
   Im vorigen Jahr waren wir für das Aufstellen des Maibaumes (may pole) *verantwortlich.*
7. I am not surprised at *(read)* Paul´s name in the newspaper.
   Waren Sie überrascht, uns hier anzutreffen?
8. You seem to be tired of *(answer)* these silly questions.
   Mein Vater hat es satt, jeden Tag so früh aufzustehen.
9. Juan and his children are tired from *(work)* in the fields all day.
   Am Abend werdet ihr vom vielen Wandern (to hike) *müde sein.*
10. I am used to *(stay)* up late and to *(study)* before an exam.
    Die Amerikaner sind es gewöhnt, viele Medaillen zu gewinnen.

6C Die Übungssätze mit den „bestimmten" Verben sind so zu behandeln wie die Sätze in **B**: *gerund* bilden, den Satz in „gutes" Deutsch übersetzen, den deutschen Satz ins Englische übertragen.

1. Mr Thompson, do you admit *(meet)* Mrs Hill on Friday and *(talk)* to her?
   Er hat zugegeben, Mrs Hill zu kennen.
2. I try to avoid *(drive)* during the rush hour, but sometimes I have to.
   Wenn du kannst, vermeide es, über das letzte Spiel zu sprechen.
3. When you have finished *(read)* the article, begin *(answer)* the questions.
   Ich fange nie vor dem Frühstück mit der Arbeit an.
4. Have you ever considered *(open)* your own business?
   Vor einigen Jahren überlegten meine Eltern ernsthaft (seriously), *unser Haus zu verkaufen und ein neues zu bauen.*
5. I met Cyril last week. – Yes, he mentioned *(speak)* with you.
   Du hast nie etwas davon erwähnt, dass du den Unfall gesehen hast.
6. Do you mind *(leave)* us alone now?
   Ich habe nichts dagegen, ein bisschen mehr zu bezahlen.
7. You risk *(hurt)* your head if you don´t wear a helmet.
   Richard riskierte, alles zu verlieren, aber er siegte.
8. Sylvia suggested *(take)* a walk after it stopped *(rain)*.
   Welcher Idiot hat vorgeschlagen, mit dem Bus zu fahren?

The Gerund

D Gerund nach *"phrasal verbs"*

Das Gerund ist **zwingend nach** bestimmten
"verb + preposition" -Kombinationen.
Solche Fügungen sind auch unter dem
Namen **phrasal verbs** bekannt.

Das sieht dann zum Beispiel so aus:
> I don´t **believe in giving** money to the poor.
> (Ich glaube nicht, dass es nützt. Ich halte nichts davon.)
> *After many experiments Edison* **succeeded in building** a grammophone.
> (Es gelang ihm, ein Grammophon zu bauen.)

Du findest hier eine Liste wichtiger **phrasal verbs**, welche das **gerund** verlangen.
Diese Liste ist – wie schon die letzte – nicht vollständig.

to apologize for	sich entschuldigen für	**to keep / prevent (sb / sth) from**	(jem.) abhalten von, hindern an
to believe in	glauben an, etw. für gut halten	**to look forward to**	sich freuen auf
to care about	sich sorgen um, sich kümmern um	**to put off**	etwas ver- schieben
to depend on	abhängen von	**to succeed in**	Erfolg haben, gelingen
to feel like	zumute sein nach	**to talk about / of**	sprechen von / über
to give up	aufgeben, auf- hören	**to thank (sb) for**	(jem.) danken für
to go / keep on	weiter(machen)	**to think about / of**	nachdenken über, denken an
to insist on	bestehen auf	**to worry about**	sich Gedanken machen über

E Gerund nach „bestimmten Wendungen"

Das Gerund ist **zwingend nach bestimmten** *"phrases"* (Fügungen,
Redewendungen).

Das sieht dann zum Beispiel so aus:
> *Dad is* **busy working** in the garden. (... arbeitet fleißig im Garten.)
> *When the film was over, Sally* **could not help crying**; it was so sad.
> (... musste sie einfach weinen. = Sie konnte nicht anders.)

(to be) busy	eifrig mit etwas beschäftigt sein	**it´s no / little use**	es hat keinen / wenig Sinn
cannot help	etwas einfach tun müssen	**it´s no good**	es hat keinen Sinn
cannot stand	nicht ertragen / aushalten können	**(is / isn´t) worth**	(nicht) wert

Tʰ**e Ge**ʳ**und**

6D Die folgenden Übungssätze enthalten *phrasal verbs*. Bilde mit den angegebenen Verben *gerunds* und übersetze die englischen Sätze, die du so erhältst, in gutes Deutsch. Danach versuche, die deutschen Sätze ins Englische zu übertragen.

1. Everything's okay now. Peter apologized for *(break)* my new pen.
   Ich bitte um Entschuldigung, dass ich zu spät komme.
2. My future depends on *(get)* this job.
3. I don't know what's wrong with me. I feel like *(cry)*.
   Mir ist heute nicht nach Lachen zumute.
4. If you want to live a healthy life, you should give up *(drink)*.
   Mein Opa gab das Autofahren an seinem 80. Geburtstag auf.
5. You can't stop now! Keep on *(try)* and one day you will succeed.
   Wir liefen weiter, obwohl wir sehr müde waren.
6. Yesterday at dinner, Caroline insisted on *(pay)* for herself.
   Mr Ericson besteht darauf, mit meinen Eltern zu sprechen.
7. Nothing in this world can keep me from *(love)* you.
8. We are looking forward to *(hear)* from you soon.
   Ich freue mich darauf, euch nächste Woche wieder zu sehen.
9. Frank, you really shouldn't put off *(talk)* to your boss too long.
10. My dad often talks about *(buy)* a little house in the country for us.
    Du sprichst immer davon, dass du weniger arbeiten wirst.
11. "Thank you for *(be)* a friend" is a wonderful song, I think.
    Danke, dass du mir geholfen hast.
12. The fight wasn't easy, but I never thought of *(give)* up.
    Denkst du auch oft daran, eine Million im Lotto zu gewinnen?
13. Don't worry about *(drive)* in the USA. They are very disciplined drivers.

6E Jeder der folgenden Sätze enthält eine *phrase*, welche das *gerund* verlangt. Finde die passende *phrase*, bilde aus dem gegebenen Verb das *gerund* und übersetze!

> *busy – worth – no use – cannot stand – couldn't help – no good*

1. I ... *(listen)* to silly people. They make me sick.
2. It's ... *(ask)* Joe. He doesn't know the answer, either.
3. It's ... *(plant)* bananas in this climate. They won't grow.
4. Forget Betty. She isn't ... *(remember)*.
5. Can you come swimming with us? – No. I'm ... *(study)* for the test.
6. I ... *(laugh)* when I saw your face. It was so funny.

7. *Es hat keinen Sinn, auf Mike zu warten. Er wird nicht kommen.*
8. *Kennst du Edinburgh? Es ist wirklich sehenswert.*
9. *Meine Eltern fahren auf Urlaub. Sie packen schon eifrig die Koffer.*
10. *Als ich „unser Lied" hörte, musste ich einfach an Max denken.*

Th**e Ge**r**und**

F Gerund nach *"instead of"* und *"without"*

Grundsätzlich kann auf jede Präposition (Vorwort, *preposition*) ein *gerund* folgen; in den meisten Fällen treten diese *prepositions* aber gemeinsam mit einem Verb als *phrasal verbs* auf (siehe Abschnitt **D**, Seite 44).

> *Lori watched the late night movie **instead of going** to bed.*
> (... anstatt / statt schlafen zu gehen.)
> *Mother left the room **without saying** a word.*
> (... ohne ein Wort zu sagen.)

G Gerund anstelle von Gliedsätzen

Das Gerund dient der **Verkürzung von Gliedsätzen**. Diese Veränderung von Satzgefügen – das ist die Kombination von Hauptsatz und Gliedsatz – führt zu „gehobenem Stil" und kommt vor allem im geschriebenen Englisch vor. Damit die „Verkürzung" funktioniert, müssen **beide Satzteile** – Hauptsatz und Gliedsatz – das **gleiche Subjekt** haben!

Von dieser „Verkürzung" sind die Zeitsätze betroffen. Sie werden mit **when**, **after** oder **before** eingeleitet. Es ist nicht wichtig, ob der Gliedsatz oder der Hauptsatz an erster Stelle steht.

> ***When* <u>Lucy</u> *came*** home from work, <u>she</u> found a telegram in the mailbox.
> ***On coming*** home from work, <u>Lucy</u> found a telegram in the mailbox.
>
> <u>The boys</u> went out to play **after <u>they</u> had done** their homework.
> <u>The boys</u> went out to play **after doing** their homework.
>
> **Before <u>you</u> jump** into the water, <u>you</u> should check its temperature.
> **Before jumping** into the water, <u>you</u> should check its temperature.

when → on	**after → after**	**before → before**

H „Indem"-Sätze → *"by" + gerund*

Die Fügung ***"by" + gerund*** entspricht den deutschen „indem"-Sätzen. Diese Sätze sagen aus, wie oder auf welche Weise etwas geschieht.

> *Mr. Vanderbilt made his millions **by building** railways across the USA.*
> (... indem er Eisenbahnen baute.)

> *Linus made Lucy very happy **by asking** her to marry him.*
> (... indem er sie bat, ihn zu heiraten.)

6F Verbinde die folgenden Sätze mit Hilfe von *"instead of + gerund"* oder *"without + gerund"*.

1. The little boy ran across the street. He did not look right or left.
2. You should not worry about Harry's plan. You should be happy about it.
3. Joe went into the house. He did not take off his shoes.
4. Irene threw the papers away. She did not read them.
5. Irene did not read the papers. She threw them away.
6. Stephen surfed the internet. He did not study French.
7. Mum watched TV. She did not iron my shirt.
8. I did all the exercises myself. I did not ask anybody for help.

6G Verkürze die folgenden Satzgefüge mit Hilfe des Gerunds. Achte dabei darauf, dass du nur die Gliedsätze durch ein Gerund ersetzt.

1. Before I leave for school in the morning, I always feed my dog.
2. Julia got many letters and telegrams after she had won the quiz.
3. When Mrs Clark heard about the fire, she broke down and cried.
4. After we had reached the top of the mountain, we took a photo.
5. Ulli checked her notes before she answered the question.
6. When the man left the hotel, he called a taxi.
7. After I had put my model plane together, I painted it.
8. I painted my model plane before I showed it to my friends.

6H Bei den folgenden Sätzen geht es um *"by + gerund"*. Verbinde die (Haupt-)Sätze mit Hilfe des Gerunds.

1. The detective solved the case. He arrested the murderer.
2. You can join our club. You must sign *(unterschreiben)* the registration.
3. A cow stopped the train. She lay down across the tracks *(Geleise)*.
4. Roberta wanted to show off to the boys. She walked on her hands.
5. Mr Brown ended the discussion. He left the room.
6. See more of the world. Join the Navy *(Marine)*.
7. "Titanic" set a new record. It attracted more people than any other film.
8. You can contact the police quickly. You must call "911".

The Gerund

Vergleiche diese beiden Sätze:

- (a) *Do you mind **opening** the window?*
- (b) *Do you mind **my** **opening** the window?*

Beide sind ganz eindeutig Gerund-Konstruktionen *(opening)*, in beiden folgt das Gerund einem „Reizwort" *(mind)*. Der unterschiedliche Sinn ergibt sich aus dem Wort *"my"* im zweiten Satz. Hier die Übersetzung:

- (a) Macht es dir etwas aus, das Fenster zu öffnen?
  - Das heißt, ich möchte, dass <u>du</u> das Fenster öffnest.
- (b) Macht es dir etwas aus, wenn <u>ich</u> das Fenster öffne?
  - Das heißt, ich möchte es öffnen und ich frage dich, ob dich das stört.

Diese Möglichkeit besteht bei vielen Gerund-Konstruktionen:
Das eingeschobene *my, your, his, her, ...* gibt dem Satz eine ganz andere Bedeutung.

Dazu noch einige Beispiele von vielen möglichen:

*I <u>dislike</u> **telling** jokes.*
  <u>Ich</u> erzähle nicht gerne Witze.

*I <u>dislike</u> **your telling** jokes.*
  Ich mag es nicht, wenn <u>du</u> Witze erzählst.

*Joe <u>is proud of</u> **winning** a prize.*
  Joe ist stolz, dass <u>er</u> gewonnen hat.

*Joe <u>is proud of</u> **my winning** a prize.*
  Joe ist stolz, dass <u>ich</u> gewonnen habe.

*We <u>are used to</u> **getting up** early.*
  <u>Wir</u> sind es gewöhnt, früh aufzustehen.

*We <u>are used to</u> **Dad's getting up** early.*
  Wir sind es gewöhnt, dass <u>er</u> früh aufsteht.

*Tim <u>worries about</u> **losing** the match.*
  <u>Tim</u> macht sich Sorgen, dass <u>er</u> das Match verliert.

*Tim <u>worries about</u> **our losing** the match*
  Tim macht sich Sorgen, dass <u>wir</u> das Match verlieren.

*Mac <u>insists on</u> **being** punctual.*
  Mac besteht darauf, pünktlich zu sein.

*Mac <u>insists on</u> **their being** punctual.*
  Mac besteht darauf, dass <u>sie</u> pünktlich sind.

 Achtung, Achtung! So wie es Verben und Fügungen gibt, die das Gerund zwingend verlangen, so gibt es auch Verben und Fügungen, auf die **nicht das Gerund, sondern der Infinitiv** folgt.

Darüber erfährst du alles Wissenswerte in Abschnitt **9G**, Seite 62.

61

Bei dieser Übung musst du mit Hilfe der vorgegebenen Verben, *phrasal verbs* usw. Gerund-Sätze bilden, und zwar immer ein Paar:
einmal mit, einmal ohne *my, your, his, ...*

Beispiel:

to talk of   →   we / visit / you

Wir sprechen oft davon, euch zu besuchen.
Wir sprechen oft davon, dass ihr uns besucht.

We often talk of visiting you.
We often talk of your visiting us.

1. to be surprised at   →   Tom / get on the team / I
   Tom war überrascht, in die Mannschaft zu kommen.
   Tom war überrascht, dass ich in die Mannschaft kam.

2. cannot stand   →   I / make fun of others / you
   Ich kann es nicht ausstehen, über andere Witze zu machen.
   Ich kann es nicht ausstehen, wenn du über andere Witze machst.

3. without   →   Dolly / win in lottery / not know about it / we
   Dolly gewann im Lotto, ohne davon zu wissen.
   Dolly gewann im Lotto, ohne dass wir etwas davon wussten.

4. to apologize for   →   Dad / be late / I
   Dad entschuldigte sich für sein Zuspätkommen.
   Dad entschuldigte sich für mein Zuspätkommen.

5. to look forward to   →   we / play "Hamlet" / he

6. to be tired of   →   I / play the trumpet / Bob

7. to be interested in   →   Jim / get to know Helen better / we

8. to hate   →   Mary / work till late at night / I

The Gerund

7 The Imperative
Die Befehlsform

Die **Befehlsform** (Imperativ) sieht **genauso** aus **wie** die **Nennform** (infinitive), die 1. Stammform des Verbs (base form), wird aber **ohne "to"** verwendet. Es gibt keine Unterschiede zwischen Einzahl und Mehrzahl oder zwischen den einzelnen Personen.

infinitive	imperative
to go, to get to open, to let to call, to write	**Go** to town and **get** some bread! **Open** the door and **let** us in! **Don't call** Joe and **don't write** him!

A Bitten, Befehle und Verbote

1. Eine **Bitte** erkennt man daran, dass sie freundlicher formuliert ist als ein Befehl. Das „Kennwort" einer Bitte ist **"please"**. Schon etwas bestimmter im Ton – noch immer kein Befehl, aber eine **Aufforderung** – ist **"will you?"**.

<u>Please</u> **hold** these books for me!
Hold these books for me, <u>please</u>!

Bitte halte(t) diese Bücher für mich!

Hold these books for me, <u>will you</u>?

Halte(t) doch einmal diese Bücher!

2. Ein **Befehl** ist viel direkter und kommt **ohne** please oder will you? aus.

Jack, **take** these books back to the library at once!
Girls, **leave** the boys alone!

3. Ein **Verbot** bedeutet, dass man etwas nicht tun darf. Das wird durch **don't + infinitive** ausgedrückt.

Harry, **don't switch on** the TV before you finish your homework.
Boys, **don't play** in the schoolyard during lessons.

B Imperativ mit "Let's …!"

Am freundlichsten ist der **Vorschlag mit "Let's …!"** oder **"Let's not …!"**

Let's wait for Jane, shall we?

Come on, boys, **let's not fight** now!

7A Sieh dir die folgenden Situationen gut an und entscheide dich dann für Bitte, Aufforderung, Befehl oder Verbot. Suche dir ein passendes Verb dafür aus.

Beispiel: *Your work is miserable, Joe. ... your parents I want to see them!*
... is miserable, Joe. Tell *your parents I want to see them!*

> get – open – bring – shut – help – tell – be – touch – tell – shoot
> call – feed – do – ask – get – let – put – shout – water – forget

1. Sammy, you're talking too much. ... quiet!
2. ... me with this exercise, please! I'm just too stupid for it.
3. Children, don't ... this machine! It can give you a shock.
4. Hey, I can't get this book down from the shelf. ... me a ladder, will you?
5. I don't know where Jerry lives. Please ... me his address! It's important.
6. When you go shopping, ... me some stamps and envelopes, please!

7. Don't ... the door if you don't know who's outside! It could be dangerous.
8. It was your mistake, not mine. So don't ... at me, will you?
9. (Mother has written a list of things for you to do)
   Monday: ... the flowers and ... the turtles!   Tuesday: ... Grandma and ... her if she needs help!   Wednesday: Don't ... to buy bread and milk!
10. (scene from a film)
    Police: "... out of the car and ... your hands on the roof!" – Man: "Don't ... me, please! I didn't do anything! You've got the wrong person! ... me go!" – Policeman: "... up and ... what I say, and you'll be fine."

The **I**mpe**r**ati**V**e

8 The Indirect or Reported Speech
Die indirekte Rede

Wenn du jemand mitteilen möchtest, was jemand anderer sagt oder gesagt hat („direkte Rede"), verwendest du die indirekte Rede. Sie umfasst Aussagen, Fragen, Befehle, Bitten und Verbote.

Bei der Bildung der *indirect speech* ist das **Verb der Redeankündigung *(reporting verb)*** von besonderer Bedeutung. Wichtige Zeitwörter in diesem Zusammenhang sind:

> ***answer – ask – complain – explain – know – mention – wonder – remember – report – say – tell – think – want to know – write***

A   Der indirekte Befehl

 Der **indirekte Befehl** umfasst von seiner sprachlichen Form her auch die **Bitte** und das **Verbot**.

Die wichtigsten ***reporting verbs*** sind ***tell*** (bei Befehl und Verbot) und ***ask*** (bei der Bitte).

 Der indirekte Befehl ist sehr einfach anzuwenden, denn zu seiner Bildung brauchst du bloß den **Infinitiv** (Nennform, 1. Stammform, ***base form***).
Es gibt auch eine zweite Art des indirekten Befehls; dabei wird aus dem Befehl (der direkten Rede) ein Aussagesatz.

* *Mitzi said (to me), "**Tidy** up your room and **go** to bed!"*   →   <u>ein Befehl</u>

  → *Mitzi <u>told</u> me **to tidy** up my room and **go** to bed.*
  *Mitzi told me / said **(that) I should tidy** up my room and **go** to bed.*

* *Mitzi said (to me), "**Don't sit** on my chair!"*   →   <u>ein Verbot</u>

  → *Mitzi <u>told</u> me **not to sit** on her chair.*
  *Mitzi told me / said **(that) I shouldn't sit** on her chair.*

* *Mitzi said (to me), "Please **help** me with my homework."*   →   <u>eine Bitte</u>

  → *Mitzi <u>asked</u> me **to help** her with her homework.*

8A Verwandle die folgenden Befehle, Verbote und Bitten in *indirect speech*. Verwende *"told"* oder *"asked"* als einleitende Zeitwörter.

1. Mr Greene: "Open your books on page 23!"
2. Father: "Go to your room and do your homework!"
3. Robert: "Take your feet off my desk!"
4. The policeman: "Get out of your car and put your hands on the roof!"

5. Gillian: "Don´t yell at me!"
6. The Coopers: "Don´t play in our garden!"
7. Vera: "Don´t write and don´t call me any more!"
8. Gus: "Don´t expect any help from me!"

9. Bill: "Please show me your photos!"
10. Willie: "Please don´t wait for me!"
11. Aunt Judy: "Come and visit us again, please!"
12. Hilary: "Don´t sell your bike, please!"

The Indirect or Reported Speech

B   Die Änderung der Zeitstufen

Wenn das **reporting verb in past tense** steht – zum Beispiel: *I asked, Tony said, we thought* –, dann kommt es zur **Verschiebung der Zeiten**; das heißt: in *indirect speech* werden andere Zeitstufen verwendet als in *direct speech*. Dabei geht man nach einem strengen Schema vor:

direct speech	indirect speech
present tense present perfect tense past tense future tense ("will")	past tense past perfect tense past perfect tense conditional present ("would")

Tony said, "**I like** New York very much. I **have** already **seen** many sights. On Sunday I **went** to Central Park. In two days I**'ll fly** home again."	**Tony said** (that) he **liked** New York very much. He **had** already **seen** many sights. On Sunday he **had gone** to Central Park. In two days he **would fly** home again.

C   Die Veränderung von Fürwörtern

Die Veränderungen der persönlichen und besitzanzeigenden Fürwörter **(personal and possessive pronouns)** ergeben sich daraus, **wer mit wem über wen spricht**.

Mac: "**I** like **your** room."   →   Mac said (that) **he** liked **my** room.
Jill: "**Bob** is **my** friend."   →   (to Bob:) Jill told me that **you** were **her** friend.

D   Die Änderung der Orts- und Zeitangaben

Sinngemäß verändern sich auch die **Orts- und Zeitangaben**, weil aus dem „Jetzt und Hier" der direkten Rede ein „Damals und Dort" in der indirekten Rede wird. Der Standpunkt des „Weitererzählers" ist anders als der Standpunkt des ursprünglichen „Erzählers".

direct speech	→	indirect speech
here	→	there
yesterday	→	the day before
today	→	that day
tomorrow	→	the next / following day, the day after
(a week, month, ...) ago	→	(a week, month, ...) before
last (week, month, year, ...)	→	the (week, month, year ...) before
next (week, month, year, ...)	→	the following (week, month, year, ...)
this	→	that
these	→	those

The Indirect or Reported Speech

8B + **8C** Übertrage die folgenden Sätze in die indirekte Rede. Leite die indirekte Rede mit einem Verb in *past tense* ein. Achte dabei besonders auf die Verschiebung der Zeiten und auf die sinngemäße Veränderung der *personal* und *possessive pronouns*.

1. Brian: "I've known Jimmy and Jerry since kindergarden."
2. Tom: "I went to Rome with Bob and Jack."
3. Maria: "Oliver and I will get married in May."
4. Norbert: "I can't find your calculator, Doris."
5. I (to Alan): "I met your parents in town on Monday."
6. Betty: "Leo and his wife are back from their holiday."
7. Aunt Maggie: "We've taken Grandma to hospital."
8. Susie: "You will like my chocolate cake."
9. Kevin: "I'm taking a shower. I can't talk to you."
10. Max: "We were not talking about you, Flora."
11. Terry: "Gunnar doesn't like his new car."
12. Esther: "My friends and I have always wanted to go to Paris together."

8D Übertrage wieder in die indirekte Rede. Dieses Mal musst du neben der Verschiebung der Zeiten und der Veränderung der *personal* und *possessive pronouns* auch noch die Veränderung der Orts- und Zeitangaben beachten.

1. Eric: "I'll meet you here after school tomorrow."
2. Dad: "Uncle Albert and I have planted five trees since yesterday."
3. Billy: "I talked to your brother an hour ago."
4. Mr and Mrs Smith: "We've just come back from our camping trip."
5. Jamie: "I found the test this morning very easy."
6. Grandma: "I'm getting nervous about your concert, Barry."
7. Mrs Gray: "Mr Gray will go on a business trip next week."
8. Man: "I bought these scales *(Waage)* last week but they don't work."
9. Our neighbours: "We have been living here since last year."

10. Publican *(Pub-Wirt)*: "You have to leave your dog outside if you want to eat here."
11. The new secretary: "I can't type very well but I can make good coffee."
12. The pop-star: "I hope I will see you all again next year."

T̲he Indirect oꝛ Reported Speech

E reporting verb in present tense

Wenn das **reporting verb in present (perfect) tense** steht – zum Beispiel *We think, Tony has said* –, dann findet **keine Verschiebung der Zeitstufen** statt. Das heißt, *present tense* bleibt *present tense* usw.
Auch die **Orts- und Zeitangaben** bleiben **unverändert**. Nur die *personal* und *possessive pronouns* **ändern sich** sinngemäß.

direct speech	indirect speech
Tony **says / has said,** "I **like** New York very much. I **have** already **seen** many sights. On Sunday I **went** to Central Park. In two days I´**ll fly** home again."	Tony **says / has said** (that) he **likes** New York very much. He **has** already **seen** many sights. On Sunday he **went** to Central Park. In two days he´**ll fly** home again.

F Fragen in der indirekten Rede

1. Für die Bildung der **indirekten Frage** ist die Art der Frage entscheidend: **Entscheidungsfrage oder Ergänzungsfrage?**

Entscheidungsfragen Antwort: JA oder NEIN	Ergänzungsfragen Antwort: ein Satzglied (Ort, Zeit, ...)
"Can I see your new room?" "Do you want to come tomorrow?" "Have you seen my brother?" "Did you call your parents?" "Will you contact us again?"	"When can I see your room?" "What do you want to do today?" "Where have you been?" "Why did you call your parents?" "How will you contact us again?"

Indirekte Entscheidungsfragen werden mit **"if"** oder **"whether"** eingeleitet. Beides bedeutet „ob".	Indirekte Ergänzungsfragen werden mit demselben **Fragewort** eingeleitet wie die direkten Fragen.
Ellen wanted to know **if** she **could** see our new room. **if** we **wanted** to come the next day. **whether** we **had seen** her brother. **if** we **had called** our parents. **if** we **would contact** them again.	Ellen wanted to know **when** she **could** see our room. **what** we **wanted** to do that day. **where** we **had been**. **why** we **had called** our parents. **how** we **would contact** them again.

2. Was ändert sich also bei der Umwandlung der direkten Frage in die indirekte?

1. Die **Zeitstufen**, die **Orts- und Zeitangaben** und die *pronouns* ändern sich entsprechend bei *reporting verb in past tense*.

2. Die indirekte Entscheidungsfrage wird mit **if / whether** eingeleitet.

3. Die indirekte Ergänzungsfrage wird mit demselben **Fragewort** eingeleitet.

8E

Übertrage die folgenden Sätze in die indirekte Rede. Achte dabei darauf, dass das einleitende Verb in *present tense* oder *present perfect tense* steht *(says / has said, tells me / has told me, ...)*.

Beachte: Du kannst in der Einleitung der indirekten Rede **"that"** weglassen.

1. The President says, "America will not give up the fight for freedom."
2. Our maths teacher has told us, "I have never seen a better class."
3. Bill writes, "I visited St. Paul's Cathedral two days ago."
4. At the end of the play Romeo thinks, "Juliet is dead."
5. Grandma remembers, "Life was hard when I was young."
6. Fred complains, "Someone has eaten my french fries."
7. Jenny explains, "I have tried to contact Brad Pitt, and now I'm waiting for an answer."
8. The newspaper reports, "Two hundred people saw the UFO yesterday."

8F

Bilde die indirekte Frage aus den folgenden Sätzen. Achte dabei darauf, ob eine Entscheidungsfrage oder eine Ergänzungsfrage vorliegt, und ob das *reporting verb* in *present (perfect) tense* oder in *past tense* steht.

1. (Jim asked us) "Have you seen a good film since last week?"
2. (Tony wanted to know) "Do you know these men?"
3. (Erica asked Carl) "Will you be at my party next weekend?"
4. (Freddy wanted to know) "Did you get this bike for Christmas?"
5. (Albert asked Victoria) "Do you want to become my wife?"
6. (Sandy asked me) "Has your dad been to America already?"

7. (the policeman wanted to know) "Where were you yesterday at 5 a.m.?"
8. (Mrs Spelling asked us) "Who has made this mess in the classroom?"
9. (Henry asked Eva) "Why didn't you ask me for help first?"
10. (I wanted to know) "When will Charlie be ready?"
11. (the little girl wondered) "How does Santa Claus know what I want?"
12. (I asked Mother) "What must I do tomorrow?"

13. (the tourist has asked us) "How can I get to the castle from here?"
14. (Gloria wonders) "When will Gerry come back?"
15. (you always ask me) "Do you know what to do next?"
16. (Bobby wants to know) "Must we do all the exercises on page 12 for tomorrow?"

The Indirect or Reported Speech

9 The Infinitive
Die Nennform

Die Nennform kennst du auch als **Infinitiv**, **1. Stammform** des Verbs oder als **base form**. Der Infinitiv kommt **mit** und **ohne "to"** vor. Weil er aber meist mit "to" auftritt, nennt man ihn auch die **"to-form"**.

A Infinitiv mit "to"

Der **Infinitiv mit "to"** ist **zwingend nach bestimmten Verben**. Die Liste hier umfasst die wichtigsten Verben dieser Gruppe.

afford	sich etw. leisten	We can't **afford to lose** this match, boys.
agree	sich bereit erklären	Joe **agreed to work** for less money.
ask	bitten	I've **asked** Tim **to drive** me home today.
decide	beschließen	We **decided to go** to Scotland next year.
expect	erwarten	I don't **expect to stay** here for ever.
happen	(zufällig)	They **happened to find** my address. (Zufällig fanden sie meine Adresse.)
hope	hoffen	I **hope to hear** from you soon!
learn	(er)lernen	Dad **learned to speak** French in Paris.
manage	gelingen, es schaffen	They **managed to put out** the fire.
offer	anbieten	Jim has **offered to drive** us home.
promise	versprechen	Will you **promise to come** back soon?
plan	planen, vorhaben	Mum is **planning to buy** a new TV.
refuse	ablehnen, sich weigern	We can't **refuse to go** to Joe's party.
seem	scheinen (als ob)	You **seem to be** sad, Margaret!
want	wollen	What do you **want to do** now, Bill?

B Infinitiv ohne "to"

Der **Infinitiv ohne "to"** kommt seltener vor, und zwar
- bei **modal verbs** (can, may, must, ...)
  *Dont't forget, Victoria. You **must call** George tonight.*
- bei **let** und **make** in der Bedeutung von „lassen" / „veranlassen" (→ **10E**, Seite 72)
  *Charlie sometimes **lets** me **use** his telefax.*
  *Dad always **makes** us **wash** the car on Saturday.*
- bei **had better (not)** = sollte lieber (nicht) und
  had rather (not) = würde lieber (nicht)
  *You'**d better leave** now or you'll miss your train.*
  *We'**d rather not walk** through the wood at night. It's scary!*
- nach **see, hear, watch** und **feel** bei schon abgeschlossener Handlung
  *Nobody **saw** us **come** back last night. (→ **16C**, Seite 96)*
  *I could **feel** the water **run** down my body.*

9A Welches Verb aus der Liste auf Seite 58 passt zu den einzelnen Sätzen?

1. I've worked very hard for this exam. Now I ... to get a good mark on it because I really can't ... to fail another exam.
2. You are an expert skier, Benny! When did you ... to ski so well? – As a child. We were living in the mountains then.
3. Where are my books, Andy? You ... to bring them back today! – I'm sorry, I forgot them again! But I ... to bring them tomorrow.
4. What's the matter with Rosemary? She doesn't ... to be herself today! – I think she is angry at Frank. He ... to go out with her last night, but he went to a bar with his friends instead.
5. Dad, what are you ... to do with your old motorbike? – Well, I've ... to sell it, and Uncle Jack has ... to buy it.
6. How did you ... to get home from school so quickly, Doris? – Well, as I was walking along Main Street, I ... to see Peter in his car. I waved to him, he stopped and ... to drive me home. I didn't ... to get here so early myself. I ... him to come in for a drink, but he said he couldn't.

Versuche, die Sätze 7 bis 12 mit Hilfe des Infinitivs ins Englische zu übersetzen.

7. George ist ein Idiot! Ich <u>weigere</u> mich, mit ihm in einem Team zu spielen.
8. Ich werde mit Daniel sprechen. Ich kenne ihn <u>zufällig</u> von der Schule.
9. Mike <u>versprach</u>, in zehn Minuten wieder da zu sein, und wir <u>erklärten uns bereit</u>, auf ihn zu warten.
10. Die Kandidatin <u>schaffte es</u>, alle Fragen richtig zu beantworten.
11. Wir <u>wollten</u> Ken <u>bitten</u>, uns bei *(with)* den Vorbereitungen *(preparations)* zu helfen, aber er war nicht zu Hause.
12 Meine Eltern haben endlich *(at last)* <u>beschlossen</u>, unser altes Auto zu verkaufen und ein neues zu kaufen.

9B Was passt zusammen? Bilde „Paare" mit den Wörtern aus den zwei Gruppen und finde den dazupassenden Satz.

> He often makes us ... – I can't ... her. –
> I saw him ... to his room. – We'd better ...! –
> We heard them ... around all night. –
> didn't let me ... to him. – We must ... with him. –
> She'd rather ... inside.

> talk – stay –
> hurry – see –
> speak – go –
> run – laugh

1. Where is Susan?
2. Look, it's 10 o'clock!
3. I know that Bill is at home.
4. Sue doesn't want to go out.
5. Have you seen James?
6. I tried to call Max, but his mum ...
7. Our German teacher is okay.
8. The boys made a terrible noise.

The Infinitive

C Adjektiv + Infinitiv

Der Infinitiv steht oft in der Kombination **adjective + infinitive**, also im Zusammenhang mit einem Eigenschaftswort.

Das sieht dann zum Beispiel so aus:

It is	**impossible**	**to know**	what Sally really wants.
Chinese must be very	**difficult**	**to learn**	for Europeans.
Mum, we are	**ready**	**to go**	!

Manchmal dient die Formel *"adjective + infinitive"* auch zur **Satzverkürzung** (und zur stilistischen Verbesserung!):

Paul was <u>sorry that he had to leave</u>. → Paul was **sorry to leave**.

D *Question word + infinitive*

Die Kombination **question word + infinitive** ist „typisch" für die englische Sprache. Mit ihrer Hilfe können wir holprig klingende Satzgebilde vermeiden und stattdessen elegante englische Sätze bilden.

I don't know <u>where I should look</u> for my glasses.
→ I don't know **where to look** for my glasses.

Joe has no idea <u>how he should programme</u> a computer.
→ Joe has no idea **how to programme** a computer.

Mary cannot decide <u>which CD she should buy</u>.
→ Mary cannot decide **which** CD **to buy**.

E Weitere Infinitiv-Kombinationen

Der Infinitiv tritt oft nach den folgenden Wörtern auf, meistens in **Verbindung mit Nomen:**

first – last – only – best – worst – enough – too (+adj.)

The first (person) **to cross** the finish line is the winner.
The captain is always **the last** (person) **to leave** the ship.
You were **the only** person / one **not to ask** for help in this situation.
I think **the best** thing **to do** now is to call a doctor.
Losing a friend is **the worst** thing **to happen**.
We had some money, but not **enough** (money) **to buy** a bigger TV.
There's not a lot of food left, but **enough to get** us through the week.
After the long illness John was **too** weak **to walk** without help.

The Infinitive

9C Suche ein passendes Adjektiv und setze es an die richtige Stelle (in Satz 1 bis 4).

1. Hermann Maier said that the race was not ... to win.
2. Laura showed us some slides *(Diapositive)* of her holiday in Italy. They were very ... to watch.
3. Doctor: "I am ... to bring you good news – nothing is wrong with your heart, Mr Smith."
4. The pictures in the film were okay, but the words were sometimes ... to understand.

   Setze nun Verben ein, die zu den vorgegebenen Adjektiven passen (Satz 5 bis 8).

5. It is good … that you are my friend, Charlie.
6. It was terrible … the news about the plane crash.
7. Little dogs are fun …
8. Tell me when you are ready …, Bob.

9D Verwandle diese „holprigen" Satzgebilde mit Hilfe der Kombination *question word + infinitive* in elegante englische Sätze.

1. Little Judy knew exactly where she should look for the Easter eggs.
2. I want to know more about astronomy, but I have no idea who I should ask for information.
3. In my dream I found myself in a room with seven doors, but nobody told me which door I should open.
4. The old man showed us what we could do with the mushrooms *(Pilze)* that we had found in the woods.
5. In driving school we learned when we had to stop and when we could go on.
6. Our chemistry teacher told us how we should conduct *(durchführen)* the experiment.

9E Verbessere die folgenden Sätze mit Hilfe einer Infinitiv-Fügung.

1. Fernando Magellan was the first European that sailed around the world.
2. As always, Ben and Steve were the last guests that arrived at the party.
3. Route 66 was the best road that you could take to California.
4. Hurricane "Andrew" was the worst storm in history that hit Florida.
5. Experts say that Fritz is the only person that understands this machine.
6. We had so much time left that we saw all the sights.
7. Carla is soooo happy that she doesn't worry about tomorrow.
8. It is so late that we can't do anything now.

The Infinitive

Verb + Objekt + Infinitiv

Die Fügung **Verb + Objekt + Infinitiv** wird im Englischen häufiger verwendet als im Deutschen. Sie sieht oft genau so aus wie im Deutschen, noch öfter entsprechen die englischen Sätze aber den deutschen **„dass-Sätzen"**.

Mr Hiller	**asked**	**me**	**to hold**	*his ladder for him.*
Uncle Mat	**wants**	**us**	**to go**	*outside and play.*
Mother	**told**	**Tim**	**to tidy up**	*his room at once.*

verb + object + infinitive

Die folgenden Verben verlangen *"verb + object + infinitive"* – eine Auswahl mit Beispielen:

advise	(an)raten	*Everybody **advises me to quit** smoking.*
allow	erlauben, gestatten	*Please **allow us to help** you!*
ask	bitten	*I **asked Tim to call** me again.*
expect	erwarten	*They **expected us to be** on time.*
help	helfen	*Who can **help them to repair** the boat?*
invite	einladen	*We **invited Bill to stay** with us overnight.*
know	wissen, kennen	*I **know you to like** sweets and cakes.*
order	befehlen	*They **ordered us to open** our bags.*
remind	(jem.) erinnern	*Please **remind Mr. Fox to call** us soon.*
teach	lehren, beibringen	*Can you **teach me to speak** Finnish?*
tell	sagen, mitteilen	*Who **told you to come** inside?*
want	mögen, wollen	*I **want Joe to stay** and **watch**.*
wish	wünschen	*Grandpa **wished me to have** his watch.*
show how	zeigen wie	*Lisa **showed Max how to do** the samba.*

Infinitiv oder *"ing-form"*?

Manchmal stellt sich die Frage, ob ein Verb eine *"ing-form"* oder den Infinitiv verlangt. Darauf gibt es mehrere Antworten. Es gibt

- Verben, die **zwingend eine *"ing-form"*** verlangen (siehe **6B** bis **D**):
z.B. *to enjoy, to mention, to give up, to think about, ...*
- Verben, die **zwingend den Infinitiv** verlangen (siehe **9A** und **B**):
z.B. *to expect, to remind, to seem, to want, ...*

The **Infinitive**

9F Übersetze die Sätze 1 bis 8 in gutes Deutsch. Was fällt dir bei den ersten vier auf, was bei den zweiten vier?

1. I advise you to stay at home in this terrible weather.
2. Mr Black allowed the children to leave ten minutes earlier.
3. Nora asked us to look after her dog while she was away.
4. The general ordered his officers to attack at dawn *(Morgengrauen)*.
5. We expect you to do your best for your friends.
6. Everybody knows me to be a talented footballer.
7. The audience *(Publikum)* wanted the band to play one more song.
8. The steward told the passengers to stop smoking.

(Richtig! 1 bis 4 weisen auch in der deutschen Übersetzung die Fügung „Verb + Objekt + Infinitiv" auf, 5 bis 8 sind „dass-Sätze".)

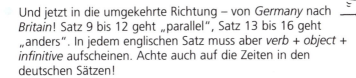

Und jetzt in die umgekehrte Richtung – von *Germany* nach *Britain*! Satz 9 bis 12 geht „parallel", Satz 13 bis 16 geht „anders". In jedem englischen Satz muss aber *verb + object + infinitive* aufscheinen. Achte auch auf die Zeiten in den deutschen Sätzen!

9. Ich rate Ihnen, das Auto jetzt zu verkaufen.
10. Philip half mir, den Text fertig zu schreiben.
11. Wir luden die Kinder ein, zum Mittagessen zu bleiben.
12. Der Polizist befahl den Leuten, aus dem Bus zu steigen.
13. Wir erwarten, dass ihr euer Bestes gebt *(do your best)*.
14. Bettina erinnerte uns daran, dass wir unsere Hausübung machen mussten.
15. Mr Jenkins teilte uns mit, dass wir morgen um 4 Uhr hier sein sollten.
16. Ich möchte, dass Conrad mit uns kommt.

9G 1. Gerund *(ing-form)* oder Infinitiv *(to-form)* – das ist hier die Frage! Setze die vorgegebenen Verben in die passende Form!

1. Everybody tells me *(come)* to Laura´s party, but I don´t want *(go)*.
2. I really don´t mind *(wait)* for a few minutes, but I can´t promise *(wait)* for half an hour!
3. Uncle Donald considered *(work)* for Mr Scrooge for a while, but then he decided *(look)* for another job.
4. Can you imagine *(leave)* your hometown and *(move)* to a big city? – No, I can´t. I´ve always wanted *(live)* where my friends are.
5. I happened *(meet)* Jennifer in a café yesterday, and I really enjoyed *(talk)* to her again.
6. Bill apologized for *(shout)* at me and he asked me *(forgive)* him. I agreed *(forget)* the whole thing.
7. I mentioned *(lose)* my bus ticket, and Janet offered *(help)* me *(look)* for it.
8. When Kurt suggested *(go)* to the cinema, I expected you *(say)* yes.

The Infinitive

2. Und es gibt auch

Verben, die **entweder *ing-form* oder Infinitiv** verlangen, und zwar		
mit **gleicher** Bedeutung	mit **geringem** Unterschied	mit **deutlichem** Unterschied
begin, continue, start, like, love, prefer, hate	*see, hear, watch, feel*	*forget, need, remember, stop, try*

ing-form = *infinitive* (→ **6A**, Seite 40)

Two masked men entered the bank and **began to fire** their guns.
Two masked men entered the bank and **began firing** their guns.
I have always **hated to work** in the garden.
I have always **hated working** in the garden.

ing-form ~ *infinitive* (→ **16C**, Seite 96)

- mit **Infinitiv** → Handlung wird „als Ganzes" gesehen; abgeschlossen.
  I **saw** you **get** in your car and **drive** off.
  We often **hear** them **come** home, **go** in and **start** a fight.

- mit ***ing-form*** → Handlung ist / war noch im Gang.
  When I looked out of the window I **saw** you **getting** in your car.
  When I can't sleep, I often **hear** you **coming** home late at night.

ing-form ≠ *infinitive*

mit **Infinitiv**	mit ***ing-form***
Sorry, Dad, I **forgot to wash** *the car again!* → notwendige Handlung (Hätte ich tun sollen!)	*I'll never* **forget washing** *it that day in the middle of the winter.* → Erinnerung an Vergangenes (Habe ich schon getan.)
We **need to paint** *the doors again.* → aktiver Zwang, Notwendigkeit (Wir müssen etwas tun!)	*The doors* **need painting** *again.* → passiver Zwang, Notwendigkeit (Es müsste etwas geschehen!)
I must **remember to tell** *you about Fred's accident.* → notwendige Handlung (Ich darf nicht vergessen!)	*Don't you* **remember telling** *me about Fred's accident?* → Erinnerung an Vergangenes (Weißt du nicht mehr?)
We ***stopped to talk*** *to the children.* → eine Tätigkeit unterbrechen, um ...	*We* ***stopped talking*** *to the children.* → eine Tätigkeit einstellen, beenden
Yesterday I **tried to ski***. It was fun.* → der echte Versuch, etwas zu tun	*You should* **try skiing***! It's fun.* → Vorschlag, Problemlösung

The Infinitive

9G

2. Fortsetzung! Du entscheidest wieder, ob *gerund* oder *infinitive* gefragt ist. Setze die passende Form ein! Überlege, wo es vielleicht zwei richtige Lösungen gibt!

1. I'd like *(see)* your homework, Barbara! – I'm sorry, sir, I forgot *(do)* it, but I promise *(bring)* it tomorrow.
2. Joe says he tried *(call)* me last night, but I don't remember *(hear)* the phone *(ring)*.
3. I can't *(open)* this box. Can you show me how *(do)* it? – Let me *(see)*! Ah, yes! Try *(put)* the key in here.
4. Why did you stop *(smoke)*? – I had to cough all the time and I could hardly climb the stairs to my apartment. So I needed *(do)* something!
5. Do you know where Miriam is? – Not really, but I saw her *(leave)* the house an hour ago, just as it started *(snow)*.
6. Did you remember *(write)* to Gradma and *(say)* thank you for the birthday present? – Yes, I did, and I apologized for not *(write)* sooner.
7. I don't remember *(see)* you here before. Are you new here? – Yes, I am. My parents want me *(go)* to school here. They expect me *(get)* better marks than in my old school.
8. Chris has been ill for two weeks now. We need *(tell)* him what's been going on here. – I happened *(talk)* to his mother two days ago. She asked me *(send)* him all the important papers because he could not afford *(miss)* too much of what we are doing.
9. I remember *(take)* the letter to the post, but Joe says he hasn't got it. I hate *(quarrel)*, but I think I need *(have)* a serious talk with him.
10. When the President entered the room, he stopped *(shake)* hands with everybody. He cannot risk *(lose)* any votes *(Stimmen)*.
11. You needn't help me with the job. I know you *(be)* an expert, but I'd prefer *(do)* it myself
12. Listen, the car is making strange noises. I think it needs *(repair)*. – I know, but I can't afford *(take)* it to a garage. – Try *(get)* George to take a look at it! If he agrees *(repair)* it, you'll save a lot of money.

10 Modal Verbs
Die Hilfszeitwörter der Aussageweise

Die Hilfszeitwörter liefern genauere Informationen über die **Art und Weise**, wie eine Handlung abläuft; zum Beispiel, ob etwas geschehen **kann**, **darf**, **muss** oder **soll**.

Die wichtigsten *modal verbs* sind **can**, **may** und **must**. Daneben interessieren uns noch die englischen Formen von **lassen** und **sollen**.

A ### can – could – to be able to

1. *"can"* entspricht dem deutschen **können, dürfen**; es gibt eine Form für *present tense (can)* und für *past tense (could)*.

2. Die **Ersatzform** von *"can"* heißt **"to be able to** + *base form"* (*"able"* heißt „fähig, in der Lage"). Mit der Ersatzform lassen sich alle Zeiten bilden; dies geschieht mit Hilfe der Formen von **"to be"**.

> We **were** able to see the show from the first row.
> **Will** you **be** able to visit me when I'm in hospital?
>   Wirst du mich besuchen können … ?
> Joe **hasn't been** able to write the programme.
>   Er hat es nicht gekonnt, er war dazu nicht in der Lage.

3. **"can / could"** drücken sowohl die **Erlaubnis** als auch die **Fähigkeit** aus; die Ersatzform **"to be able to"** steht nur bei **Fähigkeit**.

Erlaubnis	Fähigkeit
You **can go** now.	Joe **can speak** German well.
(Du kannst = darfst jetzt gehen.)	(He is able to speak it well.)
Can I **invite** Joe to my party, Dad?	**Can** you **swim**, Andy?
Joe **could drive** his dad's car.	We **couldn**'t **open** the door.
(Er konnte = durfte … fahren.)	(We weren't able to open it.)

4. Im *if*-Satz und in der **höflichen Frage** bedeutet *"could"* **könnte**. →
→ *I would help you **if** I **could**.*
→ ***Could** I see your ticket, please?*

5. Die **Verneinungen** heißen **cannot / can't** und **could not / couldn't**.

1. ***Modal verbs*** treten immer **gemeinsam mit einem Hauptzeitwort** auf – außer bei Kurzantworten oder in *tag-questions*. Das Hauptzeitwort (Vollverb) erscheint immer als ***base form*** (1. Stammform, *infinitive*), aber immer **ohne "to"**.

2. ***Modal verbs*** besitzen **nicht alle Zeitwortformen**. Es fehlen:
   ◆ die **Nennform** (*infinitive, base form*)
   ◆ die ***past form*** (2. Stammform) – mit Ausnahme von **could**
   ◆ das ***past participle*** (3. Stammform, Mittelwort der Vergangenheit)

3. ***Modal verbs*** bilden **Frage und Verneinung ohne "do, does, did".**

4. ***Modal verbs*** haben in allen Personen **gleiche Formen**. Es gibt keine unterschiedlichen Endungen (z.B. *3rd person -s*).

5. ***Modal verbs*** haben **Ersatzformen** für die fehlenden Zeiten und Formen.

10A Ersetze *"can"* und *"could"* in den Sätzen 1 bis 8 durch die passende Form von *"to be able to + base form"*.

1. I am very sorry but I cannot tell you Andrea´s address.
2. We can show you the way to the castle if you really want to know it.
3. Can you explain this maths problem to me, Phil?
4. Can anyone stop that train?
5. Uncle Tom could not walk after his accident.
6. Mr Jones could answer all our questions.
7. I thought I could do it but I couldn´t.
8. Could Ronny help you with the cooking?

In den folgenden Sätzen (9 bis 12) findest du weder *"can"* noch *"could"*. Du musst die Sätze so umformen, dass in jedem Satz „können" in irgendeiner Form vorkommt, also entweder *"can"*, *"could"* oder die passende Form von *"to be able to"*. Du musst dabei unbedingt auf die Zeit achten, in welcher der vorgegebene Satz steht.

Beispiel: *Marcus* <u>*spoke*</u> *Spanish when he was four years old.*
    (past t.)
    Marcus **was able to speak** *Spanish when ... .*

9. I <u>hear</u> you, but I <u>don´t</u> understand you.
10. Dad is sure that we <u>will beat</u> the other team tomorrow.
11. <u>Did</u> Martin sell all his records and CD´s?
12. We were so tired that we <u>did</u> not fall asleep for some time. *(2x)*

Mo**dal Ve**r**bs**

may – (might) – to be allowed to

1. Die **Ersatzform** von *"may"* heißt **"to be allowed to** + *base form"*.
"allowed" heißt „erlaubt, gestattet". Mit der Erstatzform lassen sich alle
Zeiten bilden; dies geschieht mit Hilfe der Formen von **"to be"**.

We **were** allowed to see the show yesterday.
Wir <u>durften</u> die Show <u>sehen</u>.
Will you **be** allowed to visit me when I'm in hospital?
<u>Wirst</u> du mich besuchen <u>dürfen</u>, wenn ... ?
Joe **hasn't been** allowed to use the computer.
Man <u>hat</u> es ihm nicht <u>erlaubt</u>.

2. **"may"** drückt sowohl die **Erlaubnis** (dürfen) als auch die **Möglichkeit**
(vielleicht) aus; die Ersatzform **"to be allowed to"** steht nur bei **Erlaubnis**.

Erlaubnis	Möglichkeit
You **may go** now if you want to. (Du darfst / kannst jetzt gehen ...)	Joe **may go** or he **may stay**. (Vielleicht geht er, vielleicht bleibt er. Kann sein, dass er ...)
Joe **was allowed to drive** the car. (Man erlaubte es ihm, er durfte.)	We **may drive** to town tomorrow. (Vielleicht fahren wir morgen mit dem Auto in die Stadt.)

"may" bedeutet also „vielleicht, kann sein" und kann durch *"perhaps"* oder
"maybe" ersetzt werden;
"might" bedeutet ebenso „vielleicht", ist aber noch unsicherer als *"may"*,
etwa so wie „könnte sein ...".

Beim Punkt **„Erlaubnis"** lässt sich eine Abstufung von „sehr höflich" bis
„normale Umgangssprache" feststellen.

sehr höflich **may I ?**	höflich **could I ?**	normal **can I ?**
May I say something? (selten)	Could I say something? (häufiger)	Can I say something? (üblich)

3. Die **Verneinung** hängt von der Bedeutung ab:

Erlaubnis / Verbot		Möglichkeit
sanftes Verbot (selten)	**strenges Verbot** (häufig)	**may not** **might not**
You **may not** ask.	You **must not** ask!	Joe **may not** come. He **might not** know.
... du <u>darfst</u> nicht ...		... <u>vielleicht</u> nicht ...

Modal Verbs

10B

In den folgenden Sätzen (1 bis 6) kommt *"may"* nicht vor. Du musst die Sätze so umformen, dass in jedem Satz „dürfen" in irgendeiner Form vorkommt; du brauchst also die passende Form von *to be allowed to + base form* in der richtigen Zeitstufe. Angabesatz beachten!

Beispiel: We <u>will see</u> the baby tomorrow!
          (future)
          We **will be allowed to** *see the baby tomorrow.*

1. I <u>do</u> not speak about Astrid's friends. You must ask her herself.
2. Who <u>opened</u> the first presents? – Vera was the lucky one.
3. Joe <u>has welcomed</u> the visitors. He is very proud!
4. I think I <u>would buy</u> the stereo set if I really needed it.
5. <u>Can</u> / <u>May</u> I say something? I think this is not a good plan.
6. Children under 14 <u>did</u> not see the show.

◆ Verwende *"may"* oder *"might"* statt *"perhaps"* oder *"maybe"* in den folgenden Sätzen (7 bis 12).

7. Have you done your homework, Sammy? Mr Jones will perhaps check them today.
8. My dad plays in the lottery every week. Maybe he'll win millions one day.
9. It's 10 o'clock already. Perhaps Bill won't come tonight.
10. Don't tell your dad what you did! Maybe he won't like it!
11. Have you said good-bye to the Jacksons? Perhaps they will leave for Canada next week.
12. Have you talked to Chris about the car? – No, not yet. Maybe I'll talk to him tomorrow. Why? – Well, perhaps he has sold it already. *(2x)*

◆ Erlaubt oder verboten? Bilde Sätze nach dem folgenden Muster:
Look at the photo, but don't touch it.
→ *You* **can (may)** *look at the photo, but you* **must not (mustn´t)** *touch it.*

13. Ask your friends, but don't get on their nerves.
14. Go out with Fred, but don't come home too late.
15. Have a glass of beer, but don't drink any spirits.
16. Play on the lawn *(Rasen)*, but don't damage *(beschädigen)* it.

Modal Verbs

C must – to have to

1. "*must*" entspricht **müssen**; es gibt nur die Form für *present tense*.

2. Die **Ersatzform** von "*must*" heißt "**to have to** + *base form*". Mit der Ersatzform lassen sich alle Zeiten bilden; dies geschieht mit Hilfe der Formen von "**to have**".

*Joe **had** to do all the work by himself ...*
        Joe <u>musste</u> die gesamte Arbeit alleine machen.
*... but he has done it very badly. He **will have** to do it again.*
        Er <u>wird</u> sie noch einmal machen <u>müssen</u>.

3. "*must*" und "*have to*" haben weitgehend die gleiche Bedeutung und sind daher in den meisten Fällen austauschbar.

must	have to
<u>der Sprecher selbst</u> findet eine Sache zwingend und unvermeidbar	der Sprecher will vor allem <u>eine Anordnung</u> weitergeben
*You **must try** this cake! It's great!*	*You **have to get** a haircut.*

4. Die **Verneinung** von "*must*" heißt "**do / does / did /... not have to** + *base form*" in allen Zeitstufen oder "**need not** + *infinitive without to*" (und nicht "*must not*") in *present tense*.

*It's Sunday. We **need not go** to school today.*
*Thanks, Joe, but you **didn´t have to do** this.*

D sollen

1. "**shall**" kommt fast ausschließlich in **Fragen** wie diesen vor:
        ***Shall** I show you to your room, sir?* → <u>Soll</u> ich ...
        *Where **shall** we put the bags, mum?* → Wohin <u>sollen</u> wir ...?

2. "**should**" und "**ought to**" verwendest du, wenn du jemand einen **Rat** oder **Hinweis** gibst oder jemand um Rat fragst.
        ***Should** we **know** this?* → <u>Sollten</u> wir ... ?
        *We **ought to study** for the exam.* → Wir <u>sollten</u> (eigentlich) ...

3. "**to be supposed to** + *base form*" heißt: A will, dass B etwas tut; es wird von B erwartet; B <u>soll</u> das tun.
        *Mac **is supposed to call** his parents.* → Er <u>soll</u> anrufen.
        *You **are not supposed to chew** gum.* → Du <u>sollst</u> nicht ... kauen!

4. "**had better** + *infinitive without to*" bedeutet „**sollte lieber**" (Siehe **9B**, Seite 58.)

        Modal Verbs

10C In den Sätzen dieser Übung kommt *"must"* nicht vor. Du sollst die Sätze so verändern, dass in jedem Satz „müssen" in der richtigen Zeitstufe vorkommt. Dazu musst du *"must"* oder eine passende Form von *"have to"* einsetzen.

Beispiel: *Why are you so tired, Tim? – I split all this wood here. (past t.)*
          Why ... tired, Tim? – I had to split all this wood here.

1. Where´s Agnes? – I think she <u>went</u> to the dentist.
2. Look at this! You´ve made a mess and I <u>will clean</u> it up again.
3. Grandpa doesn´t feel well. We<u>´ve called</u> the ambulance.
4. I <u>don´t</u> get up so early in summer because there´s no school.
5. Lucy came to the station with me, so I <u>didn´t</u> walk alone.
6. Look at Oscar! He <u>doesn´t</u> work today because it´s his birthday.

Was muss geschehen, was brauchst du nicht zu tun? Bilde Sätze nach dem folgenden Muster. Verwende abwechselnd *"must"* und *"have to"* beziehungsweise *"need not"* und *"(do) not have to"*.

Beispiel: *Don´t wash your feet. Wash your hands and face.*
          You need not wash your feet, but you must wash your face.
          (You don´t have to wash ..., but you have to wash ...)

7. Don´t buy a new bike. Repair your old one.
8. Don´t go to hospital. Stay in bed for some days.
9. Don´t read the whole book. Look at chapters 1 to 4.
10. Don´t spend all your money. Bring me a nice souvenir.

Setze die passende Form von „sollen" ein.

1. You *(not stay)* up so long! Think of your headache.
2. Mum says we *(come)* home before 9 p.m.
3. *(I, tell)* you what I think? I think you *(find)* a better job soon.
4. Where *(I, start)* looking for work? There are no jobs here.
5. We *(run)* faster or we won´t catch the last train today.
6. What *(I, do)* with these flowers? – They are from Gary. You *(put)* them in a vase before they wilt *(welken)* too much.
7. Peter, you *(show)* me your drawings today. Why haven´t you brought them with you? – I´m sorry, mum, but I forgot. *(I, bring)* them tomorrow?
8. *(we, tell)* Joe about the party? – No, no! It *(be)* a surprise for him!
9. We *(go)* now; Mr James is getting angry.
10. Policeman: "When I say something, you *(not talk)* back!"

Modal Verbs

E   lassen

1.   *"let"* und *"allow to"*   →   **zulassen, erlauben, gestatten**

Im modernen Alltagsenglisch kommt *"let"* häufiger vor! (Siehe auch **9B**, Seite 58.)

> *I hate these people.*   *They never **let** me **play** with them.*
> *They never **allow** me **to play** with them.*

2.   *"keep"*, *"make"* und *"force to"*   →   **veranlassen, zwingen, dazu bringen**

Hinter *"force"* steckt mehr Zwang als hinter *"keep"* und *"make"*.

> *I hate these people.*   *They always **keep** me **waiting** outside.*
> *They always **make** me **wait** outside.*
> *They always **force** me **to wait** outside.*

> *If you don't want to do it, I will **make** you **do** it!*
> *The storm **made** us **stay** inside for two days.*

3.   *have + object + 3rd form*   →   **(sich etwas) machen lassen**

Das ist eine ganz „typisch englische" Fügung, die sich von der deutschen Fassung sehr deutlich unterscheidet.
> *We always **have our car repaired** at the Opel garage.*
> Wir lassen unser Auto immer in der Opel-Werkstatt reparieren.

	have	**tea**	**served**	in the garden.
They always	**had**	**his suit**	**cleaned**	*last week.*
Dad	**have had**	**the photos**	**developed**	*!*
Look, I	**will have**	**his hair**	**cut**	*tomorrow.*
Joe	**"have"**	**object**	**past participle (3rd form)**	

> *They ...* → Sie <u>lassen</u> den Tee immer im Garten servieren.
> *Dad ...* → Dad <u>ließ</u> sich vorige Woche seinen Anzug <u>putzen</u>.
> *Look, ...* → Schau, ich <u>habe</u> die Fotos <u>entwickeln lassen</u>.
> *Joe ...* → Joe <u>wird</u> sich morgen die Haare <u>schneiden lassen</u>.

!   **Achtung! Verwechslungsgefahr** mit *present perfect tense simple*!
(Siehe Kapitel **17**, Seite 100.)
> *We <u>have repaired</u> our car.*   →   Wir <u>haben</u> es selbst <u>repariert</u>!
> *They <u>have served</u> tea.*   →   Sie <u>haben</u> den Tee (selbst) <u>serviert</u>.

„Zulassen / erlauben" oder „veranlassen / zwingen"? Entscheide dich für *"let / allow to"* oder *"keep / make / force to"*, nachdem du dir die folgenden Sätze gut angeschaut hast.

1. Did Peter ... you see his hamster? – Yes. It's lovely, isn't it?
2. Most people in my class don't like music because the teacher always ... us write so much, but we never sing.
3. Don't ... Linda use your pen! She will break it.
4. Mum will be very angry if you ... her wait with lunch again.
5. Mum will be very angry if you ... her waiting again.
6. Will you ... us to stay out until midnight, Mum?
7. They will not ... you into the house with those dirty shoes.
8. They will ... you take off your shoes before you can enter the house.

In den nächsten acht Sätzen hat jemand etwas machen lassen. Drücke das mit Hilfe der „Formel" *have + object + 3rd form* aus; beachte dabei die richtige Zeitstufe.

9. During my last visit to London I *(my picture – paint)* by a street artist.
10. Our school *(install – new computers)* next year.
11. Look, Sylivia *(her hair – dye*)*. Do you like it?
12. President Clinton always *(his picture – take)* by the same photographer.
13. We *(repair – our car)* if it wasn't so old and rusty.
14. Dad never *(his shirts – iron**)* by Mother. He always does it himself.
15. I *(never / a better picture – paint)* than this one.
16. During the holidays we *(breakfast – serve)* in our room every morning.
   * *färben,* ** *bügeln*

Die letzten acht Sätze sind eine Mischung aus allen Möglichkeiten von „lassen". Studiere die Sätze und finde die richtige Lösung.

17. They can tell me what they like, but they can't ... me change my mind.
18. If you come before the office is open, they won't ... you inside. They will ... you wait outside in the cold.
19. I must *(these notes – copy)* for the exam next week. Do you know where I can find a copy shop? – There isn't one here, but Mr Fry has a copier. I'm sure he will ... you use it if you ask him.
20. Where did you *(fix – your TV)*? – At "XXX's". But they ... us waiting for three weeks!
21. Life is a lot easier today because we can ... machines do the heavy work. – That's true. Nothing could ... me to work as hard!
22. They were very friendly at the museum. They ... us to take pictures of all the paintings and statues. – Where will you *(the films – develop)*? – At "Donald's Photo Shop", as usual.
23. I hate winter. Mum never ... me go out and meet my friends. She ... me stay inside and play with my little sister!
24. When we *(the house – built)* two years ago, we did not know that they would ... us pay so much for water and electricity.

Modal Verbs

11 The Passive Voice
Die Leideform/das Passiv

A Unterschied zwischen Passiv und Aktiv

Das Passiv und das Aktiv (die Tätigkeitsform, *the active voice*) können die selbe Sache beschreiben, aber sie unterscheiden sich in ihrer Erscheinung und Bedeutung.

passive voice	active voice
◆ **Mit dem Subjekt** des Satzes **geschieht etwas**; das Subjekt „erleidet" etwas, es ist „passiv". ◆ Das Passiv wird eher dann verwendet, wenn der **„Täter" unwichtig** oder **unbekannt** ist; nicht „wer" etwas tut ist wichtig, sondern „was" getan wird. ◆ Wenn man den „Täter" nennt, verwendet man **"by + object"**.	◆ **Das Subjekt** des Satzes **tut etwas**; es ist „aktiv". ◆ Das Aktiv wird eher dann verwendet, wenn der **„Täter" bekannt** ist; man erfährt nicht nur, „was" geschah, sondern auch, „wer" es getan hat.
<u>Gold</u> **was found** in California by some men. (Gold wurde in ... gefunden ...)	<u>Some men</u> **found** gold in California. (Einige Männer fanden Gold in ...)

B Bildung des Passivs

Das Passiv wird im Englischen mit **"to be"** + **3rd form (past participle)** gebildet. Die Form von *"to be"* richtet sich dabei nach der Zeit und nach der Person.

	passive voice – simple form			
	subject	"to be"	3rd form	
present tense	I Cheese Bananas	am is are	invited made grown	to Joe's party. from milk. in South America.
present perfect tense	The jewels My bike	have been has been	found repaired	in a stolen car. !
past tense	America The natives	was were	discovered called	by Columbus. "Indians".
past perfect t.	The doors	had been	closed	before we arrived.
future with will	The shop	will be	opened	next week.
conditional pres.	The rocket	would be	built	if it were cheaper.

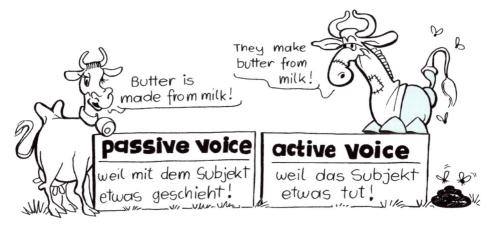

11A Übe dich im Erkennen von aktiven und passiven Sätzen. Die Frage lautet: Tut das Subjekt etwas, ist es aktiv? Oder geschieht etwas mit dem Subjekt, ist es passiv?

1. Microsoft computers are built in Seattle, USA.
2. Bill Gates founded *(gründete)* Microsoft as a young man.
3. The first computers were sold in the 1980s.
4. We have just bought a PC, too.
5. It is used by my dad, my mum and myself.
6. I play lots of games on it, ...
7. ... and I have never been beaten.
8. An internet modem will be installed soon.

11B Bilde passive Sätze *(form of "to be" + 3rd form)*. Achte besonders auf die richtige Zeitstufe.

1. A short time before the Second World War the atom *(split)* for the first time.
2. Some years later, the first bomb *(build)* by the Americans.
3. In 1945 two bombs *(drop)* on Japan.
4. Many people *(kill)* or *(injure)* by those bombs.
5. Since then, the power of the atom *(use)* to produce energy, but in several countries atomic power stations *(shut down)* again.
6. In future more power stations *(build)* all over the world and a lot of uranium *(need)* to operate *(betreiben)* them.
7. Today most of the uranium *(produce)* in Russia, China and the USA.
8. Only little uranium *(sell)* on the world market.
9. After all the questions *(answer)*, we could make a tour of the reactor.
10. We were allowed to leave the building after our clothes *(check)* for radiation.

The Passive Voice

passive progressive

In *present tense* und in *past tense* tritt das Passiv auch in *progressive form* auf. **Passive progressive** bildest du mit

"to be" + *being* + 3rd form.

present tense   →   Joe **is being interviewed** for a job at the moment.
                          (Joe wird <u>in diesem Augenblick</u> interviewt.)
                          I'm wearing shorts because my jeans **are being washed**.
                          (... weil meine Jeans <u>gerade</u> gewaschen wird.)

past tense   →   I had a cup of coffee while my car **was being cleaned.**
                          (... während mein Auto <u>eben</u> gereinigt wurde.)
                          When we arrived, the doors **were being closed**.
                          (... wurden <u>gerade</u> die Türen geschlossen.)

passive infinitive

Passive Voice kommt auch gemeinsam mit dem Inifinitiv *(infinitive, base form,* 1. Stammform) und den *modal verbs* (Hilfsverben der Aussageweise) vor. **Passive infinitive** bildest du mit

modal verb + *be* + 3rd form

can(not)   →   *Bananas* **cannot be grown** *in Central Europe.*
may (not)   →   *This film* **may be seen** *by children and grown-ups.*
must (not) →   *These boxes* **must not be opened** *before Christmas.*
should (not) →   *All questions on this sheet* **should be answered**.
need not   →   *The teachers* **need not be informed** *about this.*

Passivfügungen für neutrale Aussagen

Mit Verben, die **„sagen" und „denken"** ausdrücken, lassen sich Passivfügungen des Typs **"It is (3rd form) that ..."** bilden. Auf diese Weise bleibt der Verfasser unbekannt und ungenannt, die Aussage bleibt neutral. Dieses Passiv entspricht dem deutschen **„man-Satz"**.

believe – expect – know – report – say – think

It is known that *some Austrian wines are better than French wines.*
        (<u>Man weiß, dass</u> einige österreichische Weine ...)
It was expected that *the Canadian team would win the championship.*
        (<u>Man erwartete, dass</u> die kanadische Mannschaft ...)
It has been said that *one day computers will replace teachers.*
        (<u>Man hat gesagt, dass</u> Computer eines Tages ... ersetzen werden.)

11C

11D

Bilde passive Sätze mit den folgenden Angaben. Achte auf die Zeitstufe; einige Sätze stehen in *progressive form*, andere weisen ein *modal verb* auf, wieder andere sind „ganz normale" passive Sätze.

1. In Britain, cars should *(not park)* next to a yellow line.
2. Your moped is not finished yet. The lights *(test)* at the moment.
3. Bicycles must *(not leave)* outside overnight.
4. The match *(put off)* if it does not stop raining.
5. Mr Tompkins wants to sleep for an hour. He can *(not disturb)*.
6. Letters to the USA should *(send)* by airmail.
7. Let's talk while our things *(pack)*.
8. Look, Ronaldo *(carry)* from the football field!
9. Exercises 3 and 7 need *(not do)* for tomorrow, but for Monday.
10. "Titanic" *(see)* by more people than any other film in history.
11. During this space shuttle mission, new instruments *(test)* by NASA.
12. Hey, look at this! Your car *(tow)* away.

11E

Gestalte die folgenden Sätze mit Hilfe der nebenstehenden Verben des Sagens und Denkens so um, dass die englischen Sätze *"It is / was / … said / expected / believed / …"* enthalten.

Beispiel: *They expect Joe to go to Harvard one day.*
          It is expected that Joe will go to Harvard one day.

1. People believe that the asteroid will not hit the earth.
2. They expect Tim to give a speech tomorrow.
3. You know very well that George is the best skier in his group.
4. They have reported that all passengers survived *(überleben)* the crash.
5. They say that chocolate is good for the brain.
6. They think that the car was stolen by a young man.
7. They expect us to come to the opening of the new club.
8. Many people believe that Mrs Johnson will win the next election *(Wahl)*.

Ein Sachverhalt (Ereignis, Geschehen, ...) kann entweder aktiv oder passiv wieder-gegeben werden. Es kommt nur darauf an, **wer oder was im Mittelpunkt** der Aussage steht: „Wer hat etwas getan?" (→ aktiv) oder „Was ist geschehen?" (→ passiv).

Du musst also einen bestimmten Sachverhalt sowohl aktiv als auch passiv aus-drücken können. Eine wichtige Frage lautet daher: Wie wird **Aktiv zu Passiv** und **Passiv zu Aktiv**?

1.   *active to passive*

Subjekt	Prädikat (Verb)	Objekt	Ergänzung
The Vikings	**discovered**	Greenland	in the 10th century.
Greenland	**was discovered**	**by** the Vikings	in the 10th century.
They	**make**	good cars	in Germany.
Good cars	**are made**	——	in Germany.

1. Das **aktive Objekt** (*Greenland, good cars*) **wird zum passiven Subjekt**.

2. Das **aktive Prädikat** (*discovered, make*) **wird zum passiven Prädikat**; das heißt, es teilt sich in die entsprechende Form von **to be** und **3rd form** (*past participle*).

3. Das **aktive Subjekt** (*the Vikings, they*) **wird nur dann zum passiven Objekt**, wenn es sich dabei um jemand **Bestimmten** handelt (z.B. *the Vikings*, nicht aber *they*). Es wird mit dem Wort **by** an den Satz gebunden **(by-object)**.

4. Eventuell vorhandene **Ergänzungen** werden von diesen Veränderungen **nicht betroffen**. Sie bleiben „was" und „wo" sie sind.

11F   Verwandle die folgenden Sätze in die jeweils andere Form; das heißt, aus Aktiv mache Passiv (1 bis 8) und aus Passiv mache Aktiv (9 bis 14).

1. He defeated (*schlug*) Pete Sampras in the semifinals.
2. The Queen invites 4,000 people to her garden party every summer.
3. Look! They have renovated the old castle. It looks beautiful.
4. Francisco Pizarro and his army destroyed the Inca Empire in 1533.
5. They will present the "Oscars" in March. I wonder who will win.
6. After they had removed (*beiseite geräumt*) the tree, we could drive on.
7. The government has made pump guns illegal.
8. They will correct our tests this week. I hope I did well.

2. *passive to active*

Subjekt	Prädikat (Verb)	Objekt	Ergänzung
"Don Giovanni"	**was written**	**by** W. A. Mozart	in 1787.
W. A. Mozart	**wrote**	"Don Giovanni"	in 1787.
A new bridge	**will be built**	——	across the river.
They	**will build**	a new bridge	across the river.

1. Wenn es im passiven Satz ein **by-object** gibt, dann wird es **zum aktiven Subjekt** *(W. A. Mozart)*.
   Wenn es **kein by-object** gibt, wählt man ein **neutrales aktives Subjekt** (z.B. *they* oder *people*).

2. Das **passive Prädikat** *(was written, will be built)* **wird zum aktiven Prädikat** *(wrote, will build)*; das heißt, es **„verliert"** die Form von **to be** und das Verb wird an die entsprechende Zeitstufe angepasst (hier: *past tense* und *will-future*).

3. Das **passive Subjekt** *("Don Giovanni", a new bridge)* **wird zum aktiven Objekt**.

4. Eventuell vorhandene **Ergänzungen** werden von diesen Veränderungen **nicht betroffen**. Sie bleiben „was" und „wo" sie sind.

9. These dresses have been designed by Valentino. Aren't they beautiful?
10. Flintstone was used by primitive man to make fire.
11. Tonight the orchestra is being conducted *(dirigiert)* by Lorin Maazel.
12. The winner of the race will be announced *(angekündigt)* tomorrow.
13. When I got to the stadium, the match had been cancelled *(abgesagt)*.
14. Your name was mentioned *(erwähnt)* at the meeting yesterday.

The *Passive Voice*

G Sätze mit zwei Objekten

1. Manche englische **Sätze** weisen **zwei Objekte** auf. Anders als im Deutschen kannst du beide zur Bildung von *passive voice* heranziehen. Man nennt diese Objekte „Personalobjekt" oder „Sachobjekt", je nachdem, was sie bezeichnen.

They offer	*us*	*a bigger room.*
Gilbert gave	*me*	*his old moped.*
Lord Lucas himself will show	*you*	*the dungeon.*
	Personal-objekt	**Sachobjekt**

2. Im modernen Alltagsenglisch verwendet man in diesen Fällen viel öfter das **Passiv mit dem Personalobjekt** (was auf Deutsch nicht möglich ist!). Diese Form des Passivs heißt *personal passive.* Im Deutschen verwendet man hier die Sätze mit „man".

> **We** *are offered a bigger room.* (Man *bietet uns ein größeres Zimmer an.)*
> **I** *was given an old moped by Gilbert.* (besser: … *Gilbert's old moped.)*
> **You** *will be shown the dungeon by Lord Lucas himself.*

3. Das Passiv mit dem Sachobjekt ist auch möglich, aber in vielen Fällen nicht üblich. Es ist meist interessanter zu wissen, <u>wer</u> etwas erhält, als <u>was</u>.

> **A bigger room** *is offered us by them.*   → undenkbar!
> **An old moped** *was given <u>to</u> me by Gilbert.*   → eher nicht!
> **The dungeon** *will be shown <u>to</u> you by L. L. …*   → geht!

H Passiv aus Verb + Präposition

Aus der Kombination **verb + preposition** *(phrasal verbs)* ergibt sich eine eigene Form des Passivs: *Phrasal verbs* **dürfen nicht getrennt werden**.

> *Our neighbours* **look after** *our house when we are on holiday.*
> *Our house* **is looked after** *by our neighbours when we are on holiday.*

Hier einige Beispiele für **phrasal verbs**:

break down	(Tür) aufbrechen	**put off**	verschieben
close down	(endgültig) schließen	**put out**	(Feuer) löschen
cross out	durchstreichen	**switch on / off**	auf- / abdrehen
fill in	(Formular) ausfüllen	**take off**	ausziehen, abnehmen
knock out	niederschlagen	**throw away**	wegwerfen
look after	sich kümmern um	**try on**	anprobieren
look at	betrachten	**turn down**	leiser drehen, ablehnen
look for	suchen	**turn up**	lauter drehen
look up	nachschlagen	**wait for**	warten auf
pick up	aufheben, mitnehmen	**wake up**	aufwachen, wecken

11G Du findest hier Sätze mit zwei Objekten vor: einem Personalobjekt und einem Sachobjekt. Bilde das Passiv mit dem Personalobjekt, der weitaus häufigeren Variante.

1. They told <u>Joe</u> the whole story after some time.
2. They promised <u>me</u> a reward *(Belohnung)* for finding the lost necklace.
3. They will give <u>us</u> a bigger and better room tomorrow.
4. They have offered <u>my dad</u> a better job with more money.
5. They will show <u>you</u> how to build a tent and make a fire.
6. What do these people want? I've paid <u>them</u> for the work they've done.
7. Sue is not here. They took <u>her</u> to hospital last night.
8. Tourists often ask <u>the guides</u> silly questions.

11H Verwandle die folgenden Sätze in die jeweils andere Form, also *from active to passive* und *from passive to active*. Vergiss dabei nicht, dass *phrasal verbs* nicht „zerrissen" werden dürfen.

1. They closed down the shoe factory in 1987.
2. You must fill in all the gaps *(Lücken)* on this sheet.
3. After we had left, they switched off all the lights.
4. They will wake us at 7:30.
5. You should not throw away paper and plastic.
6. You can look up all these words in the dictionary.
7. They picked up the garbage *(Müll)* yesterday.
8. Evander Holyfield knocked out his opponent in the first round.
   (Evander Holyfield's opponent ... .)

9. The door to the hidden room was broken down by the men.
10. The concert has been put off because the pianist is ill.
11. Will your dogs be looked after when you are gone?
12. After three hours the fire was put out.
13. Shoes and hats must be taken off before you enter the temple.
14. Look, all these things have been thrown away by tourists!

The *Passive* Voice

12 The Past Perfect Tense

Die Vorvergangenheit/das Plusquamperfekt

A | **Bildung**

Die **Bildung** von *past perfect tense* ist sehr einfach und für **alle Personen gleich**.

I	**had**	**heard**	*about the band before.*
Harry	**had not**	**taken off**	*his hat before he came in.*
The boys	**had never**	**done**	*anything like this before.*
	had	**+ 3rd form**	

B | **Zeitenfolge**

 *Past perfect tense* sagt uns, **welche von** (mindestens) **zwei vergangenen Handlungen vor der** (den) **anderen** geschehen ist. Die „ältere" (erste) Handlung war dabei völlig abgeschlossen, als die „jüngere" (zweite) begann.

> *After I **had read** the book, I **took** it back to the library.*
> „ältere Handlung"   „jüngere Handlung"
> Nachdem ich das Buch <u>gelesen hatte</u>, <u>brachte</u> ich es zurück … .

> *When Dad **came** home from work, everybody **had** already **gone** to bed.*
>   zweite Handlung   erste Handlung
> Als Vater nach Hause <u>kam</u>, <u>waren</u> alle bereits zu Bett <u>gegangen</u>.

(2.) Wenn die **zwei Handlungen** aber **in der zeitlich richtigen Reihenfolge** wiedergegeben werden – also hintereinander –, wird für beide *past tense simple* verwendet.

> *I **read** the book and <u>then</u> I **took** it back to the library.*
> *Everybody **went** to bed. A little later Dad **came** home.*

C | **Vergangenheit von *present perfect simple* und *past simple***

Past perfect simple ist die **Vergangenheit** von *present perfect simple* und *past simple*. Das kommt auch in der **Zeitenverschiebung** im Rahmen der **indirekten Rede** *(indirect / reported speech)* zum Ausdruck. (Siehe dazu auch Kapitel **8B**, Seite 54.)

*We **are** tired. We **have worked** a lot.* → *We **were** tired. We **had worked** a lot.*
*Bill: "I **saw** Judy last week."* → *Bill said he **had seen** Judy the week before.*

The Past Perfect Tense

12A Vervollständige diese Sätze mit Hilfe der vorgegebenen Verben. Stelle dir vor, du hast im vergangenen Jahr deine „alte Schule" nach einigen Jahren wieder besucht; du musstest feststellen, dass sich in der Zwischenzeit allerhand verändert hatte!

1. The building looked very different. They *(build)* a new wing *(Flügel)*.
2. The old tree in the schoolyard was no longer there. It *(blow)* over in a storm and so they *(plant)* a new one.
3. I talked to Miss Roberts. She *(be)* my favourite teacher for a long time.
4. I did not see Miss Steel. She *(leave)* to teach at another school.
5. Mrs Miller was still there, but she *(become)* the new headmistress *(Direktorin)*.
6. I hardly recognised Mr Blackwell, my maths teacher. He *(change)* so much.

12B Bei den folgenden Sätzen musst du selbst erkennen, welche die „erste oder älte-re" Handlung und welche die „zweite oder jüngere" Handlung ist. Setze entsprechend *past perfect tense* (für die „ältere" Handlung) oder *past tense* (für die „jüngere" Handlung) ein.
Die Sätze mit * sollst du zusätzlich so umformen, dass die Handlungen „hinterein-ander" passieren (also beide Sätze in *past simple*).

1. Charlie *(go)* to town before I *(arrive)*.
2. The party *(go)* on for two hours after we *(leave)*. *
3. Mary *(cannot)* go out with me last weekend because she *(already, promise)* Jeremy to go out with him.
4. After I *(speak)* to my dad about the problem I *(feel)* much better. *
5. Mrs Wilson *(not know)* me because she *(never, see)* me before.
6. I *(not do)* well in the German test because I *(not have)* enough time to prepare. *
7. When the Olsons *(return)* from their holidays, they *(notice)* that someone *(break)* the livingroom window.
8. Harry *(be)* very nervous before his first date because he *(never, go)* out with Josie before.

12C Setze 1 bis 3 in die Vergangenheit und bilde von 4 bis 6 die indirekte Rede. Achte dabei auf die erforderliche Zeitenverschiebung!

1. Jack is very happy because he has found a summer job.
2. Paula doesn´t live here anymore. She has moved to Barcelona.
3. I have done all my chores *(Arbeiten im Haus)*, so we can go.
4. Valerie: "I can´t remember where I´ve put my glasses!"
5. Arnie: "Joe crashed his new car into a tree last night."
6. Francis: "We´ve never seen this woman before."

The Past Perfect Tense

Bildung von *past perfect progressive*

It	**had**	**been**	**raining**	*all night …*
You	**had**	**been**	**drinking**	*for some time …*
They	**had**	**been**	**running**	*for hours …*
	had +	**been**	**+ ing-form**	

E

Verwendung von *past perfect progressive* und *past progressive*

1. Wenn du sagen willst, **wie lange eine Handlung** schon **andauerte,
bevor eine zweite Handlung geschah**, verwendest du *past perfect progressive*.
Dabei sollte auch immer die **Zeit(spanne)** angegeben werden.

> We **had been waiting** for two hours before they **let** us in.
> Wir <u>hatten</u> schon zwei Stunden <u>gewartet</u>, bevor man uns <u>einließ</u>.

> When I **left** the house, it **had been snowing** for days.
> Als ich das Haus <u>verließ</u>, <u>hatte</u> es schon tagelang <u>geschneit</u>.

2. Wenn du aber sagen willst, dass zwei Handlungen **zum selben Zeitpunkt**
passierten (ohne Angabe, wie lange schon), musst du für die längere Handlung
past progressive verwenden.

> When I **left** the house,
> it **was snowing**.

F

Vergangenheit von *present perfect progressive*

Past perfect progressive ist die **Vergangenheit** von **present perfect progressive**. Das kommt auch in der **Zeitenverschiebung** im Rahmen der **indirekten Rede** *(indirect / reported speech)* zum Ausdruck. (Siehe dazu auch **8B**, Seite 54.)

Joe <u>is</u> tired. He <u>has been</u> working. → Joe **was** tired. He **had been** working.
Bill: "<u>I've been waiting</u> for an hour." → Bill said he **had been waiting** for …

Verben in *simple form*

Einige Verben werden grundsätzlich **nur in *simple form*** verwendet. Hier findest du eine alphabetische Liste mit einigen wichtigen Vertretern dieser Gruppe. (Siehe dazu auch Kapitel **19**, Seite 116.)

believe	*belong*	*forget*	*hate*	*have*	*hear*
know	*like*	*love*	*mean*	*need*	*prefer*
realise	*remember*	*see*	*think*	*understand*	*want*

12E

Lies dir die Sätze gut durch. Sie beschreiben in Kürze bestimmte Situationen und Ereignisse. Bilde danach Sätze mit *past perfect progressive* (Wie lange dauerte das Ganze schon, bevor … ?) und *past simple* (Was geschah dann?).

Beispiel: *Gretel was walking through the forest. After an hour she came to a gingerbread house.*
→ *Gretel* **had been walking** *through the forest for an hour when she came to a gingerbread house.*

1. The girls were playing volleyball. After ten minutes Tina scored the first point.
2. Frank went to work for General Motors. After a year he became a foreman *(Vorarbeiter)*.
3. It rained nonstop last summer. After three days and nights the river flooded our town.
4. I went to the video shop and started looking for "Armageddon". After some minutes the lady told me it was not on stock *(nicht auf Lager)*.
5. The Spice Girls began dancing and singing. Five minutes later the first people tried to climb onto the stage *(Bühne)*.

◆ Bei den nächsten Sätzen musst du entscheiden, ob die eine Handlung vor der anderen passierte *(past perfect)* oder gleichzeitig *(past progressive)*.

6. Tom was high up on a ladder. He *(look)* for a book on the top shelf.
7. Dad's hands were covered with dirt. He *(plant)* flowers in the garden.
8. Why did you look so tired yesterday? – I *(work)* all day.
9. When we came to the train station, lots of people *(wait)*. They told us they *(wait)* for twenty minutes already.

12F

Setze 1 bis 3 in die Vergangenheit und bilde von 4 bis 6 die indirekte Rede. Achte dabei besonders auf den Zeitenwechsel.

1. It smells of cigarettes! Someone has been smoking!
2. Betty is sleepy. She has been reading for hours.
3. The children are dirty all over. They have been playing in the mud.
4. Dad: "Lizzie looks frightened. I think she has been dreaming again."
5. Mum: "Drive carefully! It has been raining all night."
6. Jim: "I'm going to bed now. I've been studying all afternoon."

The *Past* Perfect Tense

13 Țḥe P̦ast Tenṣe
Die Mitvergangenheit/ das Imperfekt

A **Formen von *past tense***

Wie bei jeder Zeitstufe im Englischen gibt es auch bei **past tense** zwei Formen, **simple form** und **progressive form** (oder *continuous form).*

simple form		progressive form
regular verbs	**irregular verbs**	keine Unterscheidung in *regular* und *irregular verbs*
live**d** walk**ed** play**ed**	**wrote** **said** **took**	**was** writ**ing** **were** play**ing**
base form + (e)d	**eigene Formen**	**was / were + ing-form**

Achte besonders auf zwei **Rechtschreibregeln** beim Bilden der *past form!*

- ***y*** wird zu ***i*** bei Verben, die auf **Konsonant + *y*** enden: *stud**y** + ed* → *stud**i**ed*

- **Verdoppelung** des Endkonsonanten bei **einsilbigen** Verben: *sto**p** + ed* → *sto**pp**ed*

B **Frage und Verneinung**

Frage und Verneinung folgen in *past tense* den üblichen Regeln: Du brauchst für jede Frage und für die Verneinung ein **Hilfs(zeit)wort**. (Die Ausnahme bildet die Subjektfrage in *past simple*, die ohne Hilfswort auskommt.)

past simple	past progressive
<u>Mum</u> drank <u>juice</u> <u>in the morning</u>.	<u>At 4 p.m.</u> <u>they</u> were watching <u>a film</u>.
Did mum **drink** juice in the morning? *What* **did** mum **drink** in the morning? *When* **did** mum **drink** juice? *Mum* **did not drink** juice in the m. _{Ausnahme} *Who* **drank** juice ... ?	**Were** they watching a film at 4 p.m.? *What* **were** they watching at 4 p.m.? *When* **were** they watching a film? *They* **were not** watching a film at 4 p.m. _{Ausnahme} *Who* **was** watching a film at 4 p.m.?

Achtung!! Die Frage nach dem Subjekt steht immer in *3rd person singular*; daher fragt man in *progressive form* immer ***"Who was ...?".***

Țḥe P̦ast Tenṣe

13A Setze die folgenden Verben mit den vorgegebenen Personen in *past tense simple* und *past tense progressive*.

Beispiel: *Joe – speak*
　　　　Joe spoke – Joe was speaking

1. Bill and I – work
2. Mary – think
3. the children – play
4. it – get (cold)
5. we – try (to forget)
6. Joe – write (a letter)
7. my dad – drive (to work)
8. Sally – cry
9. Peter – bake (a cake)
10. Bill and you – dance (nicely)
11. Mr Tryon – shout (at us)
12. Susan – sleep

13B Bilde die Fragen nach den unterstrichenen Satzteilen sowie die Entscheidungsfrage *(general question)* und die Verneinung *(negation)*.

1. <u>Uncle Fred</u> bought <u>a house</u> in Glasgow <u>last year</u>.
2. <u>Nora</u> was taking <u>a shower</u> <u>in the middle of the night</u>.
3. <u>The boys</u> were watching <u>TV</u> <u>because they had nothing else to do</u>.
4. <u>Veronica</u> baked <u>a cake</u> <u>because she was hungry</u>.

Ein Freund ist eben vom Skikurs zurückgekommen, und du möchtest wissen, wie es so war. Bilde Fragen mit den folgenden Angaben (alle in *past simple*).

5. where / stay?
6. how / get there?
7. when / have breakfast / in the morning?
8. what / do / after skiing?
9. have fun?
10. the weather / nice?
11. have / a race at the end?
12. winner? *(2x)*

T̨he *P*ast Tense

Verwendung von *simple form* und *progressive form*

past simple	past progressive
(a) zur Wiedergabe von **Ereignissen aus der Vergangenheit**, die **abgeschlossen und vorbei** sind; (b) zum **Geschichten-erzählen** (*past simple* ist die „ganz normale" **Erzählzeit**);	(c) wenn **zu einem bestimmten vergangenen Zeitpunkt gerade eine Handlung im Ab-laufen** war; (d) wenn **zwei oder mehrere Handlungen gleichzeitig abliefen** (meist *while*-Sätze); (e) wenn **eine Handlung noch andauerte, als eine andere Handlung begann** (kurze Handlung = *past simple,* unterbricht lange Handlung = *past progressive*; meist *when*-Sätze).

(a) *Yesterday my brother Tim* **found** *a handbag on his way home from work.*

(b) *He* **opened** *it and* **looked** *inside. There* **was** *some money and a piece of paper with a name and an address on it. Tim* **went** *to the address, …*

(c) <u>*At 5 o'clock yesterday afternoon,*</u> *Tim* **was walking** *home through the park. The sun* **was shining***, a soft wind* **was blowing** *and a few clouds* **were moving** *across the sky.*

(d) <u>*While*</u> *Tim* **was crossing** *the large meadow, he* **was thinking** *of the weekend. People* **were sitting** *in the grass* <u>*while*</u> *little children* **were playing** *everywhere.*

(e) *Tim* **was bending** *down to get one of the children's frisbees* <u>*when*</u> *he noticed the handbag.*

Verben in *past simple*

Einige Verben werden **nur in *past simple*** verwendet. Hier findest du eine alphabetische Liste mit wichtigen Vertretern dieser Gruppe. (Aber Achtung! Es gibt auch Ausnahmen* von dieser Regel! Sieh dazu besonders unter **18D**, Seite 115 nach!)

believe	belong	forget	hate	have*	hear
know	like	love	mean	need	prefer
realise	remember	see*	think*	understand	want

Große **Verwechslungsgefahr** besteht zwischen **past tense** und **present perfect tense** (vor allem bei *simple form*).
Alles Wesentliche dazu erfährst du unter **17K**, Seite 110.

The Past Tense

13C

13D

Entscheide dich für *past simple* oder *past progressive*. Streiche die falsche Variante durch.

1. When the alarm clock *went / was going* off this morning, I *slept / was sleeping* soundly *(fest)*.
2. I *got / was getting* up and *walked / was walking* to the bathroom.
3. While I *took / was taking* a shower, mum *prepared / was preparing* my breakfast.
4. We *had / were having* tea and toast with jam.
5. I *packed / was packing* my schoolbag when the doorbell *rang / was ringing*.
6. It was my friend Gerry. He *asked / was asking* me if I *wanted / was wanting* to walk to school with him.
7. I *said / was saying* yes, and five minutes later we *left / were leaving*.
8. When we *got / were getting* to the bus stop, all our friends *waited / were waiting* for the bus, too.

In den nächsten acht Sätzen geht es nur um die Punkte (c) bis (e). Entscheide dich wieder für *past simple* oder *past progressive*.

9. We *(walk)* home when it *(begin)* to rain.
10. I *(read)* an exciting story when the lights *(go)* out.
11. When Mum *(look)* out of the window this morning, it *(snow)*.
12. What *(your sister, do)* yesterday afternoon at 6 o'clock? – I think she *(study)* for an exam in her room.
13. Everybody *(read)* their newspapers while they *(wait)* for the train.
14. *(you, ski)* very fast when you *(fall)* and *(break)* your leg?
15. Bernie *(take)* my photo album while I *(look)* in the other direction.
16. I *(do)* the dishes when somebody *(knock)* on the window.

„Zwei Handlungen gleichzeitig" oder „eine nach der anderen"? Entscheide dich wieder für *past simple* oder *past progressive*.

17. When Joe *(arrive)*, we *(look)* at his holiday photos.
18. When Joe *(arrive)*, we *(have)* dinner. We couldn't wait for him.
19. I *(see)* Terry in the café this morning. He *(sit)* at his usual table and *(read)* the morning papers.
20. Last night I *(take)* a shower when the telephone *(ring)*. So I *(dry)* myself, *(go)* downstairs and *(answer)* the phone. It *(be)* Tom. He *(want)* to know what I *(do)* at the moment.
21. Yesterday Dad *(get)* his car back from the garage. While he *(drive)* home, he *(hear)* a strange noise. It *(come)* from the engine. So he *(stop)* the car, *(open)* the bonnet *(Motorhaube)*, and what *(he, find)*? A screwdriver which the mechanic had forgotten.
22. At the beginning of the lesson I *(not know)* what the teacher *(talk)* about, but after I while I *(understand)* most of it.
23. When Tony was young, he *(hate)* potatoes but he *(like)* spinach.
24. Eric *(tell)* me that the big Mercedes *(belong)* to him now. He had bought it the week before.

The Past Tense

14 The Possessive Case

Der 2. (besitzanzeigende) Fall

Der zweite Fall (Genitiv, *genitive*) zeigt die **Besitzverhältnisse** oder die **Zugehörigkeit** an. So wissen wir, wem oder zu wem etwas gehört.

A Auskunft über die Besitzverhältnisse

Das **besitzanzeigende Fürwort** gibt klare Auskunft über diese Besitzverhältnisse.

Du erfährst **alles Wesentliche** über *possessive pronouns* in **Kapitel 20B**, Seite 120.

B *Saxon genitive*

Den **zweiten Fall mit ...´s oder ...s´** nennt man manchmal auch den *Saxon genitive*, weil er ein Überbleibsel aus der Zeit der Angelsachsen ist. Er kommt **im Wesentlichen** nur **bei Personen** vor, aber es gibt auch Ausnahmen von dieser Regel.
Beim Schreiben kommt es darauf an, wo der **Apostroph** („das Stricherl") steht – beim Reden merkt man allerdings keinen Unterschied.

Pluralwörter, die **auf „s"** enden: **...s´**	Wörter, die **nicht auf „s"** enden: **...´s**
my friends´ house (meiner Freunde) *This is the Millers´ new car.*	*my friend´s house* (meines Freundes) *the children´s toys*

Die **„Ausnahmen"** betreffen:

Eigennamen auf -s:	**Lukas´s** *parents*	*the* **Jones´s** *house*
(Haus-)Tiere:	**our cat´s** *rubber ball*	*the* **dog´s** *place*
Länder und Städte:	**London´s** *buses*	*the* **United States´** *flag*
Entfernungen	**a mile´s** *journey*	
und Zeitangaben:	**an hour´s** *walk*	
einige *"phrases"*, z.B.:	**today´s** *news*	**life´s** *dark sides* usw.

C Der Genitiv mit *"of"*

Die **häufigste Form** des 2. Falls ist der Genitiv mit *"of"*. Du kannst ihn grundsätzlich immer verwenden, aber bei Personen und Eigennamen klingt *Saxon genitive* besser!

> *I like the colour* **of** *your hair.*
> *Dad cut off the branches* **of** *the tree.*
> *Aber:* **Frank´s mother** *statt the mother of Frank*

14B Bilde den passenden zweiten Fall. Verwende *Saxon genitive*, wo es möglich ist. Achte dabei besonders auf die Stellung des Apostrophs.

14C Beispiel: *Dad has a car. It is green.*

  Dad's car *is green. (Green is* the colour of *Dad's car.)*

1. The bus has two doors. They are too narrow.
2. Max has lots of friends. They are very funny.
3. Bob has new skis. They are carvers.
4. Our house is at number 11, Jefferson Street. *(The address …)*
5. This is Linda. Her telephone number is 456-7890.
6. The girls need new shoes. Their shoes are too small.
7. The man has lost his hat. The wind blew it away.
8. The drive to Salzburg takes one hour.
9. This is the newspaper. It came yesterday.
10. The Underground in London is called *the tube.*
11. New York has many sights. They are very interesting.
12. "Godzilla" has been the biggest flop this year.
13. My cat has a little rubber mouse. This is it.
14. The United Kingdom has a beautiful flag. It is called the "Union Jack".
15. This cheese has a strong smell. I don't like it.
16. Tom has a little dog. It is called "Boxer".

17. My car doesn't start. Something is wrong with the engine.
18. Uncle Simon has a valuable *(wertvoll)* stamp collection.
19. Mr and Mrs Miles have a flower shop. It is in the High Street.
20. This is a list with the concerts next month.

The *Possessive* Case

15 Prepositions

Vorwörter/Präpositionen

Die wichtigste **Aufgabe** einer Präposition besteht darin, eine **Beziehung zwischen einem Verb und einem anderen Satzteil** herzustellen.
Der Sinn einer Aussage ändert sich nämlich beträchtlich, wenn man die Vorwörter austauscht:

*Look, Brenda is sitting **at / under / behind** her desk.*

Beziehungen, die durch Vorwörter hergestellt werden		
wo? *prepositions of place*	**wann?** *prepositions of time*	**Sonstiges** *"other" prepositions*
at, on, in, under, next to, below, off, ...	for, till, before, after, at, from ... to, since, ...	with, without, about, against, for, from, ...

Da es keine „Regeln" für die Anwendung der Präpositionen gibt und die meisten Präpositionen mehr als eine Bedeutung haben, solltest du dir Vorwörter immer **im Zusammenhang mit einem Verb oder einem Nomen** merken, zum Beispiel: **on** the wall, **in** the picture, to look **for**, to consist **of**, ...

 A | ### Zeitangaben

Dieses „Zeitlineal" erklärt die wichtigsten **Vorwörter der Zeit (prepositions of time)**.

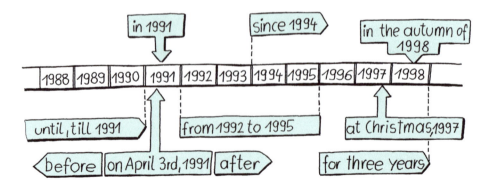

Die Zeichnung mit dem „Vogelhaus" enthält alle wesentlichen **Vorwörter des Ortes *(prepositions of place)***. Sie erklären dir „wo, woher und wohin".

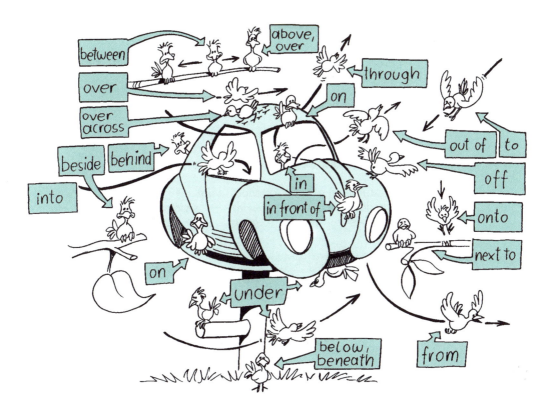

15A Löse die folgenden Aufgaben mit Hilfe des „Zeitlineals".

1. We lived in the country *(bis 1989)*.
2. *(am 3. April 1989)* we moved into a big apartment in town.
3. *(1989)* I started going to a new school.
4. I had been to a very small country school *(vor 1989)*.
5. *(von 1990 bis 1993)* Mr Brown was my English teacher.
6. He was my English teacher *(vier Jahre lang)*.
7. *(seit 1992)* my little sister has been going to the same school.
8. I went back to the place in the country *(zu Weihnachten 1995)*.

15B Bilde Sätze mit den Präpositionen im „Vogelhausbild" nach diesem Muster:

> *The bird is flying* into *the birdhouse. – ... sitting* on *the roof.*

*P***r***epositions*

16 The Present Participle

Das Mittelwort der Gegenwart

Das *present participle* ist das Mittelwort der Gegenwart (1. Mittelwort, Partizipium Präsens). Es ist eine **"ing-form"** des Verbs.

Du bildest das *present participle* nach der „Formel"

> **base form + ing**

Dabei musst du auf **drei Rechtschreibregeln** achten:

 Wegfall des „stummen e" am Wortende: *write* → *writing*
 Verdoppelung des Endkonsonants: *swim* → *swimming*
„Verwandlung" *-ie* zu *-y*: *lie* → *lying*, *die* → *dying*, *tie* → *tying*

A Bildung

1. Das **present participle** ist **Teil der progressive form**, die nach der folgenden „Formel" gebildet wird:

> **"to be" + present participle**

 2. Dabei passt sich die Form von *"to be"* an Person und Zeitstufe an, während das *present participle* seine Form nicht verändert:

	is going	to a football match. Look, there he is!
	was going	to a football match when we saw him.
Joe	**has been going**	to football matches since he was six years old.
	had been going	to football matches for years before I met him.
	will be going	to football matches ten years from now.

Genaue Informationen über Bildung und Gebrauch der *progressive form* findest du in den Kapiteln zu den einzelnen Zeitstufen und in Kapitel **19**, Seite 116.

B Verwendung als Adjektiv

Das **present participle** dient **als Adjektiv** (Eigenschaftswort, *adjective*) zur näheren Beschreibung eines Nomens (Hauptwort, *noun*). (Vergl. Kap. **1**, Seite 8.)
> We booked a room with **running** water.
> Everybody felt sorry for the **crying** boy.

16A Bilde von den folgenden Verben die *progressive form*. Achte dabei auf die vorgegebene Zeitstufe und Person.

Beispiel: *we dance* → *we are dancing*

1. Joe smokes (a cigar)
2. you wrote (to Grandpa)
3. Jenny has waited (long enough)
4. I will talk (to a large group)
5. they would call (if they knew our number)
6. it had rained (all night)
7. the children swim (in cold water)
8. we lay (on the beach)

16B Setze die *present participles* an passender Stelle ein.

> *boring – sitting – whispering – running – losing – driving – falling – interesting – dancing*

1. "... Man" is a Stephen King book and an Arnold Schwarzenegger film.
2. In the Battle at Little Big Horn River, the Sioux under "... Bull" beat the US Army under General Custer.
3. One of my favourite songs is *"Listen to the Rhythm of the ... Rain."*
4. What an ... book! Have you read it too? – Yes, but I think it was ...
5. It was a ... battle *(Schlacht)* from the first moment on. We couldn't win.
6. In the story, Cinderella put on her ... shoes and went to the King's ball.
7. In English, the name of the river would be *"... Water"*.
8. When I'm eighteen, I'll get my ... licence *(Führerschein)* and buy a car.

The Present Participle

Das „typisch Englische" am *present participle* ist sein **Auftreten mit bestimmten Verben** und seine Eigenschaft als „**Satzverkürzer** und **Satzverknüpfer**".

 ## *present participle* nach Verben der Sinneswahrnehmung

Nach **Verben der Sinneswahrnehmung** folgt oft das *present participle*. Dabei dauert die beschriebene Handlung meist noch an, sie kann aber auch schon abgeschlossen sein. In beiden Fällen kann nach dem Verb auch ein Infinitiv stehen. Vergleiche dazu auch Kapitel **9B**, Seite 58.

> ### feel – hear – notice – see – watch

> I <u>felt</u> the cold water **rising**. (oder: I <u>felt</u> the water **rise**.)
> We <u>heard</u> you **coming** home last night. (oder: ... **come** home ...)

 ## Zwingender Gebrauch

Nach **go, come, keep** und **catch** folgt zwingend ein *present participle*.

> Who wants to **go skating** on the weekend?
> Two fire engines **came racing** along the motorway. There must have been an accident somewhere.
> Please don't **keep** me **waiting**! I'm in a great hurry!
>   Bitte lass mich nicht warten. (Siehe auch **10E**, Seite 72.)
> Mrs Hillerman **caught** us **copying** from the book.
>   Sie erwischte uns beim Abschreiben.

 ## Verknüpfung von Handlungen

Mit Hilfe des *present participle* lassen sich **gleichzeitige Handlungen verknüpfen**. Voraussetzung dafür ist allerdings, dass alle Handlungen **dasselbe Subjekt** aufweisen.
Die Handlung mit dem *present participle* wird dabei zur „Nebenhandlung"; die „<u>Haupt</u>handlung" steht im <u>Haupt</u>satz.

> Bob <u>sat</u> (was sitting) in the bathtub. He <u>whistled</u> (was whistling) a song.
> **Sitting** in the bathtub, Bob <u>whistled</u> / <u>was whistling</u> a song.
> Bob <u>sat</u> / <u>was sitting</u> in the bathtub **whistling** a song.

 ## Unmittelbar aufeinander folgende Handlungen

Bei **unmittelbar aufeinander folgenden Handlungen** kann die erste Handlung durch ein *present participle* ausgedrückt werden. Voraussetzung: Beide Handlungen weisen **dasselbe Subjekt** auf!

> George <u>took off</u> his boots and <u>went</u> into the living room.
> **Taking off** his boots, George <u>went</u> into the living room.

The Present Participle

16C

16D

Wähle aus den vorgegebenen Verben ein passendes aus, bilde das *present participle* und setze es an geeigneter Stelle ein. Damit die Sache leichter wird: Jedes Verb soll nur einmal verwendet werden.

> *laugh – get – run – walk – dance – rise – try –*
> *guess – plant – go – wait – climb – drive*

1. I saw you ... flowers in your garden yesterday. Don´t you think it's too early for that?
2. We heard you ... out last night. Where did you go? – To a disco. Tony and I always go ... at the weekend.
3. Joe fell and broke his leg when he came ... down the stairs after someone had knocked at the door.
4. A few days ago Joe noticed some men ... into the neighbours´ house through the kitchen window. He knew the neighbours were not at home because he had seen them ... in their car and ... away. So he called the police, and they caught the men ... to run away with the neighbours´ TV.
5. I watched you ... up and down outside the cinema in the rain. Why didn´t you go in? – We couldn´t! They kept us ... until ten minutes before the film started.
6. What a sad story! I can still feel the tears *(Tränen)* ... to my eyes!
7. What a stupid mistake! I can still hear the people ... at me.
8. (patient to doctor) Please tell me what's the matter with me. Don´t keep me ... !

16E

16F

Baue in die folgenden Sätze mindestens ein *present participle* ein.
Bei gleichzeitig ablaufenden Handlungen sind auch zwei Mittelwort-Fügungen möglich. Versuche beide!

1. Pat was sitting by her desk. She was studying for an exam.
2. We stood outside the supermarket. We waited for Herbert.
3. Mum was lying on the sofa. She was talking to Aunt Liz on the phone.
4. Joe and Jill walked up the hill. They told each other jokes.
5. We looked at the posters. We waited for the film to begin.
6. I thought of Simon. I looked at some old photos.
7. Dad opened his umbrella and walked out into the rain.
8. I turned around and noticed a stranger. He was following me.
9. Bill put on a warm coat and went outside to play with his friends.
10. Mary read the telegram and asked me if she could help.
11. Henry left the house and waved back *(winkte)* at his wife.
12. The dog climbed out of the water and shook himself dry.

The Present Participle

present participle anstelle eines Gliedsatzes

Das *present participle* kann einen **Gliedsatz ersetzen**, der mit **after, as, when** oder **while** eingeleitet wird. Das ist eine sehr elegante und stilvolle Ausdrucksweise, die man im gesprochenen Englisch nicht oft hört.
Dabei müssen nur die Sätze, die mit *while* eingeleitet werden, in Hauptsatz und Gliedsatz dasselbe Subjekt aufweisen.

   gleiches Subjekt in Gliedsatz und Hauptsatz:

> As Joe does not like *animals very much, he never looks after our dog.*
> **Not liking** *animals very much, Joe never looks after our dog.*

> While Bill was walking *home from work, he was thinking of his girlfriend.*
> **Walking** *home from work, Bill was thinking of his girlfriend.*

> After the plane had landed, *it rolled towards the hangar.*
> **Having landed**, *the plane rolled towards the hangar.*

(oder mit *gerund* → *After landing, the plane rolled ...*)
(oder der letzte Schrei im Alltagsenglisch → eine Kombination:
   After having landed, the plane rolled ...)

   verschiedene Subjekte in Gliedsatz und Hauptsatz:

> As *the rain* **got** *heavier and heavier, the tourists decided to stay inside.*
>   **S1**   **S2**
> *The rain* **getting** *heavier and heavier, the tourists decided to ... .*

> After *Joe* **had said** *what he wanted to say, the meeting was over.*
> *Joe* **having said** *what he wanted to say, the meeting was over.*

present participle anstelle eines Relativsatzes

Das *present participle* kann in einigen Fällen einen **Relativsatz (relative clause)** ersetzen.

> People *who live* in the desert are used to heat and dust.
> People **living** in the desert are used to heat and dust.

> Have you noticed the picture *that hangs* in Joe's office?
> Have you notice the picture **hanging** in Joe's office?

Mehrere *present participles* in einem Satz

Ein einzelner Satz kann auch **mehr als ein *present participle*** enthalten. In diesem Fall bleibt nur das Verb des Hauptsatzes (mit der „Haupthandlung") erhalten.

> As I *was looking* for a certain book, I *found* a letter that *was lying* on the floor.
> **Looking** for a certain book, I **_found_** a letter **lying** on the floor.

                                                  The Present Participle

16G Ersetze die Gliedsätze durch *present participles*. Beachte dabei besonders das Subjekt des Gliedsatzes!

1. When I walk home from school, I always pass by Mr Nelson´s toy shop.
2. While Joe was visiting New York City, he made a day trip to Washington.
3. As Mum was tired after the dinner party, she went to bed early.
4. After Bill had watched a film about Greenland, he decided to study geology and geography.
5. As we were driving along in my car, we were listening to Will Smith´s latest songs.
6. While Kevin was working last summer, he met Lisa. They are still friends.
7. As Cathy did not know what to do, she called the information desk.
8. After the rain had stopped, the open air concert continued.
9. As Jack was late again, we went to the concert without him.
10. After the guests had left, we cleaned up the living room.
11. As Helen had a fever, we brought her some pills from the chemist´s.
12. After Uncle Edward had lost all his money at roulette, his familiy had to sell their big house and move to a smaller one.

16H Ersetze den Relativsatz *(who ..., that ...)* durch ein *present participle*.

1. Do you know the men who are talking to Joe over there?
2. The correspondents who are reporting from Cairo will return next week.
3. Joe was woken up by the telephone that was ringing beside his bed.
4. The bridge that crosses the river between here and Westfield has to be torn down and rebuilt.
5. Is there anybody who wishes to talk to Mr White?
6. The people who live next door to us have moved here from Russia.

16I In einige der folgenden Sätze kannst du mehr als ein *present participle* einbauen. Damit es leichter wird, ist in den ersten zwei Beispielen das „Haupt-Zeitwort" unterstrichen.

1. When Erica came home from work yesterday, she <u>saw</u> a stranger who was running away from her house. As she felt quite frightened, she called the police at once.
2. While we were driving through Scotland, we <u>noticed</u> lots of sheep grazing *(weiden)* beside the road. As we like animals very much, we stopped and took a few snapshots.
3. As we were late, we took the train that was waiting on the nearest track *(Gleis)*. Unfortunately it was the wrong one.
4. While Paula was waiting for the bus, she studied the posters that were covering the walls of the waiting room.

The **P**resent **P**arti**c**iple

17 The Present Perfect Tense
(Die Vergangenheit)

Present perfect tense wird oft mit der deutschen Vergangenheit (dem Perfekt) gleichgesetzt, aber das stimmt nur zum Teil und führt zu Missverständnissen.

A | Bildung von *present perfect tense*

1. So sehen die **Formen von *present perfect tense*** aus:

present perfect simple	present perfect progressive
I, you, we, they **have asked** *he, she, it* **has asked**	*I, you, we, they* **have been asking** *he, she, it* **has been asking**
have / has + 3rd form	**have / has been + ing-form**

2. **Fragen und Verneinung** werden ohne weiteres Hilfswort direkt mit **have** oder **has** gebildet; die Frage nach dem Subjekt heißt immer "*Who has …?*"

> **Have** you **asked** Joe? – We **haven't asked** Joe. – Who **has asked** Joe?

B | Verwendung von *present perfect simple*

Present perfect simple beschreibt Handlungen, die – meist erst kurz – vor dem „Jetzt und Hier" passiert sind, aber **Auswirkungen und Folgen auf die Gegenwart** haben. Eigentlich erfahren wir etwas über das „Jetzt"!
Es ist dabei **unwichtig, wann** die Dinge geschehen sind (vor einem Jahr oder vor wenigen Sekunden); **wichtig** ist, **dass** sie geschehen sind und dass sie etwas mit der Gegenwart – mit dem „Jetzt und Hier" – zu tun haben.

> Joe **has arrived**. → Joe ist da, und daher können wir („jetzt und hier")
> mit dem Essen beginnen, ins Kino gehen oder
> zu Hause bleiben, ihn ausfragen usw., usw., …

> We **have found** the key. → Hauptsache, er ist wieder da! <u>Jetzt</u> können
> wir wieder ins Haus hinein oder weggehen und
> absperren oder …

> Jill **has gone** to town. → Sie ist (jetzt) leider nicht da!

> **Have** you **done** your homework? → Bist du (jetzt) fertig?
> Können wir jetzt etwas anderes tun?

17A Setze die Beispiele 1 bis 4 in *present perfect simple* und 5 bis 8 in *present perfect progressive*.

1. The cat *(catch)* a mouse.
2. Valerie *(find)* the love of her life.
3. We *(pass)* the exam. We are very happy.
4. You *(not finish)* your chores *(Arbeiten im Haus)*.
5. It *(snow)*. The mountains are white.
6. Why are you so dirty? – We *(play)* outside.
7. Rosie *(lie)* in the sun. Now she has a sunburn.
8. What *(you, do)*? You look tired. – I *(play)* squash.

Bilde mit den folgenden Sätzen die Fragen nach den unterstrichenen Satzteilen, die Entscheidungsfrage und – in Satz 9 – auch die Verneinung.

9. <u>Peter</u> has lost <u>all his money</u>.
10. <u>The children</u> have been playing <u>catch</u> <u>outside</u>.

17B Was hat zu diesen Situationen geführt? Stelle dir Ereignisse vor, die vor kurzem passiert sind und diese Folgen haben.

Beispiel: *Ben doesn't live here any more. (find / new apartment)*
    → *He has found a new apartment.*

1. Jane is in hospital. *(have / baby)*
2. I feel much better now. *(start / jogging)*
3. You can't go with Bill. *(leave / with Monica)*
4. I have to walk home from school now. *(someone / take / bike)*
5. Look, Anne's hair is orange! *(dye* / it)*   * färben
6. Bobby can't walk. *(break / leg)*
7. Dad is very upset. *(lose / car key)*
8. You can't speak with Mr Black. *(leave / office)*
9. Doris is not in town. *(go away / on a holiday)*
10. We know the story. *(read / the paper)*
11. Walter lives in Chester now. *(they / offer / better job)*
12. We can go on now. *(they / repair / car)*

The Present Perfect Tense

C Bezug zur Gegenwart

Present perfect stellt immer einen **Bezug zur Gegenwart** her *(present tense)*. Manchmal verwendet man ***"just"*** und ***"already"***, um diesen Bezug noch zu verstärken.

just „soeben, gerade"	**already** „schon, bereits"
Dad **has** <u>just</u> **called**. He's coming.	Good! I**'ve** <u>already</u> **made** his dinner.
Would you like a drink? –	
No, thanks, I**'ve** <u>just</u> **had** one.	No, thanks, I**'ve** <u>already</u> **had** one.
Do you know where Bob is? –	
I think he **has** <u>just</u> **left**.	I think he**'s** <u>already</u> **left**.

D Zeitraum reicht bis in die Gegenwart

Wenn du über einen **Zeitraum** sprichst, **der bis in die Gegenwart reicht** – also bis „jetzt" – , dann verwendest du ***present perfect simple***. Der Zeitraum, der dabei gemeint ist, wird **nicht ausdrücklich genannt** – aber der Sprecher und der Zuhörer wissen, was gemeint ist (z.B. die Jahre in der Schule, das ganze bisherige Leben, der Urlaub bis jetzt, ...). Oft (aber nicht immer) verwendet man in diesem Zusammenhang ***"ever?"*** und ***"never"***.

ever? „schon (einmal)?, jemals?"	**never** „nie(mals), noch nie"
Have you <u>ever</u> **seen** "Pulp Fiction"?	→ No, I'**ve** <u>never</u> **seen** it.
How many times **has** Fritz **been** to Great Britain or Ireland?	→ He **has** <u>never</u> **been** there.
Have you <u>ever</u> **smoked** a pipe?	→ Yes, but I'**ve** <u>never</u> **tried** cigars.

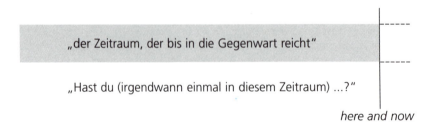

„der Zeitraum, der bis in die Gegenwart reicht"

„Hast du (irgendwann einmal in diesem Zeitraum) ...?"

here and now

17C Bei den folgenden Sätzen musst du passende Antworten mit *"just"* und *"already"* finden. Meistens passen beide Antworten! Zwei Beispiele:

(a) *Have you heard from Joe? (call)* → *Yes, he* has just called.

(b) *Can you call Joe now? (talk)* → *But I* have already talked *to him.*

1. Are you hungry, Bill? *(eat)*
2. When are you going to pay the bill, Tom? *(call / waiter)*
3. Would you like to go to the cinema with me? They are showing "Casablanca" with Humphrey Bogart and Ingrid Bergman. *(see)*
4. Where is Bob? *(he, leave)*
5. Don´t forget to tidy up your room, Mollie. *(do it)*
6. Why don´t you ask your mother where your red dress is? *(find it)*

17D Bilde Fragen mit *"ever"* und Antworten mit *"No, but ..."* bei den Sätzen 1 bis 6.
Beispiel: *(you) see / the Eiffel Tower? – visit / the Tower of London.*
Have you ever seen *the Eiffel Tower? – No, but* I´ve visited *the Tower of London.*

1. (you) collect / stamps – build / model planes
2. (Joe) live / in a big city – spend / a few weeks / in New York
3. (the children) read / any German books – read / many English ones
4. (you) learn / a foreign language – visit / many foreign countries
5. (your parents) build / a house – buy / the house that we live in
6. (you) drive / a sports car – sit / in one

Bilde Aussagen mit *"never"* und *"but I have already / often / sometimes ..."* bei den Sätzen 7 bis 12.
Beispiel: *(you) visit / the Tower – see / the Eiffel Tower*
I have never visited *the Tower, but* I´ve already seen *the Eiffel Tower.*

7. (I) go out / Mary-Jean – often / talk / her
8. (Bob) play / polo – already / ride / horse
9. (the girls) act / in a play – sing / in a choir
10. (Frieda) be / to Italy – travel / through France
11. (some old people) see / the ocean – make / a boat trip / on a river
12. (we) try / whisky – taste / beer

Einengung des Zeitraums

Manchmal will man den „**Zeitraum**, der bis an die Gegenwart heranreicht", **einengen**, sodass er nicht das ganze Leben, die bisherige Schulzeit, den Urlaub bis jetzt, ... umfasst, sondern eben nur **„vor kurzem, unlängst, in letzter Zeit"** meint. Dafür verwendet man *present perfect simple* gelegentlich sogar mit einer Zeitangabe:

> **in the last few (minutes, hours, days, ...)** (in den letzten paar Minuten, ...)
> – **recently** (in letzter Zeit, vor kurzem) – **so far** (bis jetzt)

> **Have** you **heard** anything of Joe? I **haven´t seen** him in a long time.
> – Yes, I´**ve met** him <u>recently</u>. He looks fine.

> How do you like your new car? **Have** you **had** any problems <u>so far</u>?
> – No, everything´s fine.

> **Has** Joe **called** you <u>in the last few days</u>?
> – No, we **haven´t heard** from him <u>recently</u>.

F

Weitere Zeitangaben mit *present perfect simple*

Man verwendet auch **die folgenden Zeitangaben mit *present perfect simple***, wenn sie **noch nicht abgeschlossen** sind.

> **today – this morning (afternoon, week, month, ...)**

> **Has** anybody **seen** Mike <u>today</u>?   (→ Der Tag ist noch nicht zu Ende!)
> Yes, I´**ve talked** to him <u>this morning</u>. (→ Der Vormittag ist noch nicht
>   vorbei! Es ist noch vor 12 Uhr.)

Wenn der Sprecher aber zum Beispiel um 15 Uhr sagen würde, dass er Mike heute schon gesehen hat – und zwar am Vormittag (der dann ja schon vorbei ist!) –, dann müsste er **past simple** verwenden, also "Yes, I **talked** to him this morning" sagen.

> Alles Wesentliche über den Unterschied zwischen *present perfect* und
> *past* erfährst du in Abschnitt **17K**, Seite 110!

"yet" und "not yet / already"

Für die Frage „Hast du **schon ... ?**" und die Antwort „**nein, noch nicht / ja, schon**" verwendest du *present perfect simple* mit **"yet?"** und **"not yet / already"**.

> **Have** you **heard** from Joe <u>yet</u>?   (Hat er sich <u>schon</u> gemeldet?)
> – No, he **hasn´t called** <u>yet</u>.   (Nein, hat er <u>noch nicht</u>!)
> – Yes, he **has** <u>already</u> **called**.   (Ja, er hat <u>schon</u>.)

> Joe **hasn´t told** Julia <u>yet</u> that he loves her, but he is going to do it tonight.

17E Bilde Fragen und Antworten mit *present perfect simple* und einer passenden „Zeitangabe". (+ bedeutet *yes*, – bedeutet *no*)

17F Beispiel: *(you) write / to Kevin* (in den letzten Wochen)
+ *(I) send / letter* (vor kurzem)
Have *you written* to Kevin in the last few weeks?
Yes, *I* have sent *him a letter* recently.

1. (you) see / Herbert *(vor kurzem)* ?
   – (we) not see or talk to him *(bis jetzt)*
2. (your father) go / on holiday *(in den letzten Monaten)* ?
   + (he) be / fishing *(vor kurzem)*
3. (you) read / newspaper *(heute)* ?
   – (I) not have / time *(heute Morgen)*
4. (anybody) use / my computer *(heute Nachmittag)* ?
   + (Greg) type / some letters on it *(vor kurzem)*
5. (the children) do / the shopping *(heute)* ?
   – (they) not come back / school *(bis jetzt)*
6. (you) have / any contact / with Americans *(heuer)* ?
   + (we) show / some tourists around the town *(in den letzten Wochen)*
7. (anybody) speak / with Bob / about his schoolwork *(in letzter Zeit)* ?
   – (I) not see / him *(in den letzten Tagen)*
8. (you) touch / this machine *(in den letzten paar Minuten)* ?
   – (I) not be / inside this room *(bis jetzt)*

17G Bilde Fragen mit *"yet"* und Antworten mit *"no, not yet"*, *"no, not so far"* und *"yes, already"*.

1. you / talk to your parents / about London trip – no / have no time / so far
2. you / ask Mary / for telephone number – no / not talk / yet
3. Joe / tell you / about his accident – yes / I / sign / his plaster cast
4. you / meet / Paul – yes / we / speak

   Antworte auf die Fragen und sage, was jemand noch nicht gemacht hat, was er / sie aber bald machen wird.

Beispiel: *Have you made a fire, Joe?*
I haven´t made a fire yet, but I´m going to make it now.

5. Have you packed your suitcases? – pack them now
6. Has Uncle Willy sold his old car? – buy a new one
7. Has Grandma seen Wendy´s baby? – we, visit her next week
8. Has Charlie had ice-cream? – order one soon

The Present Perfect Tense

present perfect progressive beschreibt zwei Arten von Handlungen

länger dauernde Handlungen, die erst vor kurzem zu Ende gingen;	längere Handlungen, die „jetzt und hier" noch andauern;
das sind die deutschen **„die ganze Zeit"**–Sätze (mit Verb im <u>Perfekt</u>)	das sind die deutschen **„schon seit ..."**–Sätze. (mit Verb im <u>Präsens</u>)
You look tired. What's the matter? **I have been studying.** (Ich <u>habe die ganze Zeit gelernt</u>. Aber jetzt lerne ich nicht mehr.)	*You look tired. What's the matter?* **I have been studying** <u>for hours</u>. (Ich <u>lerne schon seit</u> Stunden. Und ich lerne noch immer!)
*Why are your shoes wet? – Don't you know? It **has been raining**.* (Es hat die ganze Zeit geregnet, aber jetzt regnet es nicht mehr.)	*Why are your shoes wet? – Well, look! It **has been raining** <u>since five in the morning</u>.* (Es regnet schon seit fünf Uhr früh und es regnet daher noch immer.)

Aufpassen musst du auch bei der Frage
    What have you **been doing?** → Was hast du denn die ganze Zeit gemacht (z.B. seit wir uns das letzte Mal sahen)?

    What have you **done** (to your shoes)? → Was hast du denn (mit deinen Schuhen) gemacht? (z.B. weil sie so schmutzig sind)

"since or for"?

Present perfect progressive sagt uns auch, **seit wann** oder **wie lange** eine Handlung andauert. Wir brauchen daher eine **Zeitangabe**, die uns das mitteilt, entsprechend dem deutschen **„schon seit ..."**.
Dafür gibt es im Englischen zwei Wörter: *"since"* und *"for"*.

since <u>seit</u> einer bestimmten <u>Zeit</u> („damals") bis „jetzt und hier"	*for* eine bestimmte <u>Zeit lang</u> bis „jetzt und hier"
since **6 o'clock** since **last night** since **yesterday** since **last Sunday** since **January** since **1995** since **the 17th century**	for **two minutes** for **half an hour** for **ten days** for **six months** for **twenty years** for **a long time** for **ever**

17H Was ist passiert? Sieh dir die folgenden Situationen an. Bilde dann die Frage und sage – beides mit Hilfe von *present perfect progressive* –, was vorher („die ganze Zeit über") los war.

Beispiel: *Dad has come in from the garden with dirty hands. – (dig)*
What has *he* been doing? *– He's* been digging.

1. Andrew's clothes are full of sand. – *(build – sandcastle)*
2. Susan has got a red nose. – *(wait – in the cold)*
3. You look exhausted *(erschöpft). – (jog – along the beach)*
4. The boys have blisters *(Blasen)* on their hands. – *(play – "tug-o´-war")*
5. Kathy's eyes and cheeks are red. – *(cry)*
6. Joe is sleeping. – *(work hard)*
7. Bill looks like falling asleep. – *(drive – all night)*
8. Mary looks so happy. – *(talk to her boyfriend)*
9. You are looking at me so strangely. – *(think about you)*
10. The children's clothes are soaked *(durchnässt). – (make – a snowman)*
11. Fred is very red on his back. – *(sunbathe)*
12. Harry has a bloody nose and Bill is missing a tooth. – *(fight)*

17I Bei den folgenden Sätzen sollst du sagen, wie lange / seit wann „das schon so geht".
Beispiel: *Dad is digging in the garden. He started digging an hour ago.*
Dad has been digging in the garden for an hour.

1. Melanie is learning Greek. She started learning Greek last year.
2. Police are looking for a stolen car. They started looking for it on Monday.
3. The Millers are staying here. They arrived here three days ago.
4. Jack's dad works in Ireland. He started working there in 1997.
5. Stanley and Oliver play the piano. They started playing the piano when they were five years old.
6. Brian is studying for his final exam. He began studying in March.
7. I am waiting for Sylvia. I got here at 9:30.
8. Fred is out jogging. He left here 45 minutes ago.
9. Claire is crying. She started crying ten minutes ago.
10. The children are watching TV. They switched on the telly at 3 p.m.
11. My grandparents live in the country. They moved there a long time ago.
12. Lukas's dad writes books. He started writing books in 1980.

The Present Perfect Tense

Unterschied zwischen *present perfect simple* und *present perfect progressive*

Present perfect simple und *present perfect progressive* unterscheiden sich in etlichen Bereichen. Hier siehst du eine **Gegenüberstellung** der zwei Formen.

present perfect simple have / has + 3rd form	*present perfect progressive* have / has + been + ing-form

Zustände	Handlungen
<u>How long</u> **has** Joe **been** married? – He has been married for a year.	<u>How long</u> **has** Joe **been working** for this company? – He has been working for them for a year.
How long **have** the boys **been** here? – They have been here since last week.	How long **have** the boys **been staying** here? – They have been staying here since last week.
Wie lange <u>ist</u> er schon <u>verheiratet</u>? Wie lange <u>sind</u> sie schon <u>hier</u>?	Wie lange <u>arbeitet</u> er schon ... ? Wie lange <u>wohnen</u> sie schon ... ?

meist **Handlungen**, die **schon sehr lange andauern**	meist **Handlungen**, die **erst seit kurzem andauern**
Dad **has worked** for his company <u>for ever</u>.	Dad **has been working** for his company <u>for half a year</u>.
We **have lived** in this house <u>since I can remember</u>.	We **have been living** in this house <u>since last summer</u>.

Ergebnisse, Folgen mit oder ohne Zeitangabe	Handlungen mit oder ohne Zeitangabe
The door was shut, now it is open. Someone **has opened** that door.	Joe **has been looking** for his door key. He can't get into the house.
I**'ve read** two books <u>this week</u>. They were quite interesting.	I**'ve been reading** this book <u>for two weeks</u>. It's not very interesting.

<u>Ausschließlich</u> *present perfect simple* kommt in Frage	
wenn etwas „**seit ...**" oder „**so lange**" **<u>nicht</u>** oder **noch nie** geschehen ist.	bei **bestimmten Verben**. (Eine alphabetische Liste findest du in Abschnitt **19**, Seite 117.)
I **<u>have not</u> seen** Brenda for two days. We **haven't talked** to our neighbours since last week. Joe **<u>has never</u>** drunk alcohol.	Es heißt daher zum Beispiel: I **have known** Jim for many years. und nicht: I have been knowing him for many years.

17J *Present perfect simple* oder *progressive*? Entscheide dich für eine der zwei Formen und setze sie ein.

1. How long *(your neighbours, be)* on holiday? – For a week. They *(go)* to Turkey.
2. My elder sister *(study)* medicine at university for two semesters, but she *(not take)* a single exam yet.
3. My dad *(drive)* to work since before I was born, but in the last few days he *(take)* the bus because his car *(break)* down. The mechanics *(try)* to repair it for days but they *(not find out)* yet what the problem is.
4. I *(know)* Jacqueline for three years, but we *(be)* in the same class only for two years.
5. Hi, Joe! Do you want to come to the cinema with me? – No, I can't! You see, I *(count)* my picture post cards. So far I *(count)* these three boxes, and there are three more to count. I *(not do)* this in a long time. I wonder how many I have got.
6. Steven Spielberg *(make)* a few superb films recently. *(you, see)* any of them? – Yes, I *(see)* "Jurassic Park" and "J. P. The Lost World", but I *(not have)* the chance to see "Saving Private Ryan" yet.
7. Julia is a great traveller. She *(already, visit)* more than forty countries on all continents, but she *(not be)* to China yet. Now she is in Argentina. She *(travel)* round South America for two months now.
8. There are splashes of white paint in your hair and face! What *(you, do)*? – I (paint) my room, but I *(not finish)* yet. – How much *(you, paint)* already? – Only the ceiling and one wall.

Sieh dir die folgenden Situationen an und reagiere mit Aussagen, Fragen, ... mit der passenden Form von *present perfect tense*.

9. You look thinner than last time, Doris. *(you, lose)* weight?
10. Would you like a cigarette, Mary? – No, thanks, I *(not smoke)* since Christmas.
11. *(you, ever, speak)* with a really famous person? – Yes, with Madonna. I *(know)* her since my stay in Los Angeles. We *(be)* in contact since then.
12. Look, it *(snow)*! Everything is covered in white! – Great! When did it last snow here? – A long time ago! It *(not snow)* for more than three years.
13. I did well in my last maths test but I *(not study)* for the next test yet. *(you, look)* at the examples yet? – Oh yes, I *(work)* on them for two days and I *(already, do)* more than half. They aren't very difficult.
14. Look at Edward! Why is he so excited? – I think he *(watch)* thrillers again! – Eddie, what *(you, do)*? – I *(just, finish)* watching "The ABC Murders". What a great film!
15. Why has Mr Arrows got greasy *(ölig, fettig)* hands? – He *(repair)* Louis's bike. The chain *(Kette)* *(break)* and Mr Arrows *(order)* a new one.
16. Next day: Louis, you can ride your bike again. Mr Arrows *(repair)* it for you! – Thanks, Mr Arrows. I *(never, meet)* a nicer man!

The Present Perfect Tense

past simple oder *present perfect simple?*

Verwechslungsgefahr besteht auch bei *past simple* und *present perfect simple*, vor allem für uns Deutschsprechende. Uns ist es egal, ob jemand sagt:

> „Ich habe gestern meine Schlüssel verloren"   oder
> „Ich verlor gestern meine Schlüssel."

Wir wissen auf jeden Fall, was gemeint ist. Wir erkennen bestenfalls an Ausdrucksweise und Wortwahl, aus welchem Teil des deutschsprachigen Gebiets der Sprecher kommt. Vielleicht bemerken wir auch noch einen Unterschied im Stil. An der Aussage ändert das nichts!

Ganz anders im Englischen! Hier besteht ein großer Unterschied zwischen

past simple	present perfect simple
*"I **lost** my keys"*	*"I **have lost** my keys"*
sagt uns nur, dass er sie <u>irgendwann einmal</u> (zum Beispiel: gestern) verloren hat; wir wissen nicht, ob er sie noch immer vermisst, oder ob er sie inzwischen schon gefunden hat. Wir erfahren also etwas über das „Damals", nicht über das „Jetzt".	sagt uns etwas über das „Jetzt" – der Arme kann im Augenblick nicht über seine Schlüssel verfügen, weil er sie verloren hat. Der Zusatz *"yesterday"* ist uninteressant (und nicht möglich); der Sprecher will uns nicht mitteilen, <u>wann</u> er die Schlüssel verloren hat, sondern <u>dass</u> er sie verloren hat.

2. Dieser grundsätzliche Unterschied macht sich in den folgenden Fällen bemerkbar:

irgendwann einmal	gilt aber „jetzt" nicht mehr, weil ...
Bob **won** a lot of money in the lottery, Joe **shaved** his head, but	but he **has spent** it all. (Er ist pleite.) his hair **has grown** back again.

„historische" Ereignisse ohne Bezug zur Gegenwart	Ereignisse mit Bezug zur Gegenwart
*How many plays **did** Schiller **write**?* (Schiller ist tot! Er kann keine Stücke mehr schreiben! Daher → historisch!)	*How many books **has** John Grisham **written** (so far)?* (Grisham lebt und hat es bisher auf 6 Bücher gebracht. → Bezug zu „jetzt")
*Who **invented** gunpowder? – The Chinese, of course, 3000 years ago.*	*Bill Gates **has invented** a new operating system for his computers.*

vergangener Zeitpunkt abgeschlossener Zeitraum	Zeitraum bis „jetzt"
*I **saw** five musicals <u>last year</u>. <u>As a child</u> Joe **lived** in the country.*	*I **have seen** three musicals <u>this year</u>. He **has lived** here <u>for 10 years</u> now.*

ZWISCHENÜBUNG

Bilde mit den vorgegebenen Personen und Verben jeweils

- *past tense, simple* und *progressive form*
- *present perfect tense, simple* und *progressive form*

Beispiel: *Joe – study French*

Joe studied French Joe has studied French
Joe was studying French Joe has been studying French

1. Paul and Paula – take dancing lessons
2. I – practice for the concert
3. we – do all the work in the house
4. William – go out with Helen
5. Mum – work as a nurse
6. the storm – blow

17K

Present perfect oder *past*? Überlege die Zusammenhänge und wähle die richtige Zeitstufe.

1. How many bottles of beer *(you, drink)* last week? – Last week? I think I *(have)* five beers. – And this week? How many *(you, have)* this week? – Only two so far.
2. I'm sorry I'm late again. How long *(you, wait)* for me? – About ten minutes. But don't worry, yesterday I *(wait)* much longer.
3. Today is a special day. My parents *(be)* married for fifteen years! They *(meet)* at university while both *(be)* students there and *(get)* married soon after.
4. Before Uncle Tom *(come)* to this town, he *(live)* and *(work)* in Scotland. Now he *(live)* here for twenty years, and he *(work)* for the same people for ten years.
5. Look at this weather! It *(rain)* for three days now. – Terrible, isn't it? But last week *(be)* worse! It even *(snow)* one time, but the snow *(not stay)* for long.
6. *(you, see)* James recently, Eve? – Well, I *(go)* out with him on Friday evening, but I *(not see)* him since then.
7. What a nice car, Veronica! When *(you, buy)* it? – Last week. But I *(not drive)* around a lot yet.
8. My dad's brother *(buy)* a weekend house on the coast some years ago, but he *(sell)* it again because it *(be)* too expensive.

The Present Perfect Tense

18 The Present Tense
Die Gegenwart/Präsens

Wie jede Zeitstufe im Englischen tritt auch *present tense* als **simple form** und als **progressive form** (auch *continuous* oder *expanded form*) auf. Es ist nicht gleichgültig, welche Form man für verschiedene Aussagen verwendet.

 ## A Formen von *present tense*

present simple		present progressive		
I, you, we, they	**ask**	I	**am**	**asking**
He, she, it	**asks**	you, we, they	**are**	**asking**
		He, she, it	**is**	**asking**

Auf keinen Fall darfst du das **-s** in *3rd person singular (he, she, it)* vergessen! Wenn der Infinitiv *(base form)* auf einen Zischlaut endet, hängst du in der dritten Person oft **-es** an und sprichst [iz] – *wash**es**, wish**es**, guess**es***.

 ## B Frage und Verneinung

Frage und Verneinung folgen in *present tense* den üblichen Regeln: Du brauchst für jede Frage und für die Verneinung ein **Hilfs(zeit)wort**. (Die Ausnahme bildet die Subjektfrage in *present simple*, die ohne Hilfswort auskommt.)

present simple	present progressive
Mum drinks *tea every day*.	*Jill and Ian* are watching *TV right now*.
Does mum **drink** tea every day?	**Are** they watching TV right now?
What **does** mum **drink** every day?	What **are** they watching right now?
When **does** mum **drink** tea?	When **are** they watching TV?
Mum **does not drink** tea every day.	They **are not** watching TV right now.
• Who **drinks** tea every day?	• Who **is** watching TV right now?

Achtung!! Die Frage nach dem Subjekt steht immer in *3rd person singular;* daher fragt man in *progressive form* immer **"Who is ...?"**.

The Present Tense

18A Setze die Beispiele 1, 2, 3 und 8 in *present simple* und 4 bis 7 in *present progressive*.

1. My parents and I always *(talk)* about my problems.
2. My mother often *(get)* angry, but my dad always *(let)* me say what I *(want)* to say.
3. I *(like)* my brother and my brother *(like)* me, but sometimes we *(fight)*.
4. Hey, you *(sit)* on my chair! Get up and let me sit down.
5. Look, Mr Smith *(run)* to the bus stop. He is late again.
6. I can´t come with you now. I *(write)* my homework.
7. The boys *(play)* hide and seek. I can´t see them.
8. Sometimes my brother *(wish)* that he was older.

18B Frage nach allen unterstrichenen Satzteilen und bilde die Entscheidungsfrage und die Verneinung. Achte dabei auf die Person in der Angabe.

1. In the west of Ireland it rains every day.
2. Uncle Ernest drives a school bus on Monday and Tuesday.
3. My grandparents live in a small village.
4. Joe goes to bed at 8 o´clock because he needs a lot of sleep.
5. I love working in the garden in summer because it is fun.
6. The French drink lots of coffee in cafés and at home.
7. Robert and I are going to town to meet Jill in the library.
8. Father is painting the doors and windows.
9. Gerda´s parents are reading the newspaper in the livingroom.
10. My sister and I are driving to Switzerland over the weekend.
11. My boyfriend is waiting in front of the school.
12. Harry and Sally are going home because they are tired.

The *P*resent Tense

present simple	present progressive
(a) bei **zeitlosen Zuständen und allzeit gültigen Tatsachen**;	**(d)** bei **Handlungen, die zum jetzigen Zeitpunkt passieren** (oder noch nicht abgeschlossen sind);
(b) bei **regelmäßigen** oder **wiederholten Handlungen**;	
(c) bei **zukünftigen Ereignissen**, die **zeitlich genau festgelegt** sind (siehe auch Kapitel 5D, Seite 38).	**(e)** bei **zukünftigen Handlungen in Verbindung mit einer Zeitangabe** (siehe auch Kapitel 5C, Seite 38).

(a)   Bananas **grow** best in tropical countries.
Water **boils** at 100° C or 212° F.

(b)   Mum and Dad **leave** the house at 8 o'clock every morning.

(c)   Martha's plane **arrives** at 4:25 tomorrow afternoon.

(d)   Look, there are Joe and Tim. They **are going** to the sports centre.

(e)   **Are** you **coming** to Bill's grill party on Saturday?

D   Einige Verben werden nur in *present simple* verwendet

Hier findest du eine alphabetische Liste mit wichtigen Vertretern dieser Gruppe. Aber Achtung! Es gibt auch Ausnahmen* von dieser Regel!

believe	**belong**	**forget**	**hate**	**have***	**hear**
know	**like**	**love**	**mean**	**need**	**prefer**
realise	**remember**	**see***	**think***	**understand**	**want**

Es muss heißen:	und nicht:
Now I **know** the answer.	Now I ~~am knowing~~ the answer.
This album **belongs** to me now.	It ~~is belonging to me now.~~

* zu den Ausnahmen: *have, see* und *think* kennen sowohl *simple form* als auch *progressive form*, wenn auch bei geänderter Bedeutung:

I **have** 246 different stickers.	≠	We **are having** lunch now.
(besitzen)		(essen)
We **see** Amanda every day.	≠	I **am seeing** her to the bus stop now.
(sehen)		(begleiten)
Leo **thinks** you will come.	≠	We **are thinking** of inviting you ...
(denken, vermuten)		(etw. überlegen, an etw. denken)

18C *Present simple or present progressive?* Wähle die passende Form.

1. The sun *(rise)* in the east and *(set)* in the west. That's a law of nature.
2. The Jacksons *(leave)* for Portugal next Friday. They *(spend)* two weeks there every year.
3. Richard *(say)* he *(read)* an interesting book at the moment. I *(want)* to read it, too, when he has finished it.
4. Dad's train *(leave)* from track 17 in fifteen minutes. He *(go)* to Hamburg on business. Usually he *(fly)* but this time he *(take)* the ICE.
5. Uncle Joe is a very reliable *(verlässlich)* person. He always *(remember)* to write me a birthday card and he never *(forget)* to put a £ 5 note in it. But this year he himself *(come)* to my birthday party.
6. George says he *(go)* to the disco on Friday, but I *(not believe)* him; he never *(go)* to discos because he *(not like)* to dance.
7. Look, it *(rain)* and I *(not have)* my umbrella with me. – You can take mine, I *(not need)* it at the moment.
8. Hello, Jack! What *(you, do)* here? I haven't seen you for a long time. – Hi, Bob! I *(visit)* my sister. – *(she, still, live)* in your parents' house? – Yes, but she and her husband *(build)* their own house at the moment.
9. Why *(Oliver, run)*? – He *(want)* to catch the bus. He always *(take)* the bus at 8:10 and it *(always, be)* on time.
10. Terry *(stay)* with his parents at the moment, but he *(look)* for his own place to live. When he *(find)* it, he will move out.
11. We *(go)* to Egypt this summer! – Really? That's great! We *(learn)* about Egypt in school at the moment. – What *(you, know)* about it? – Well, for example, that the River Nile *(flow)* into the Mediterranean Sea.
12. Helen, *(you, come)* to Diana's garden party on Saturday? – I *(not think)* so. We always *(visit)* my parents in the country on Saturday, and this Saturday we *(leave)* early.
13. Is Norman a good driver? – No, but he *(learn)*. I *(teach)* him.
14. This robot *(work)* faster than ten people, but at the moment it *(not work)* at all. It broke down yesterday afternoon.

18D *Present simple or present progressive?* Entscheide!

1. This walkman *(belong)* to Marcus. – Oh, now I *(understand)* why he *(not let)* me use it.
2. What *(you, think)* Dad will say when he *(hear)* about your problems at school? – I *(not know)*! Usually we *(try)* to discuss these things, but sometimes he *(get)* angry, too.
3. You *(look)* happy, Petra. What's the matter? – I *(think)* of Peter. He is sooooo nice! He *(take)* me out again on Saturday. We *(go)* to a pizzeria and then to a disco.
4. Mr Udall says he *(own)* six houses, but I *(not believe)* him. I *(think)* he *(lie)*. – Why? *(you, know)* him? – Yes, and he never *(tell)* the truth.
5. What *(your dad, do)*? – He *(work)* for a bank. But at the moment he *(not work)* because he has had an operation and he can't sit.
6. Listen! Somebody *(try)* to get into the house! – That's Felix, our cat. He always *(make)* that noise.

The Present Tense

19 Progressive Form & Simple Form

Zwei „typisch englische" Formen des Zeitwortes

In den Kapiteln über die einzelnen Zeitstufen – *present tense, present perfect tense, past tense, past perfect tense* und *future* – erfährst du alles Wesentliche über *simple form* und *progressive form* der jeweiligen Zeitstufe.

Hier findest du eine **Zusammenfassung** und einen **Überblick** über die zwei Zeitwortformen, die für die englische Sprache so typisch sind.

simple form	*progressive form*
Erklärung der Begriffe	
Simple form bedeutet <u>einfache Form</u>. Sie heißt deshalb so, weil sie **ohne Erweiterungen** – eben ganz „einfach" – gebildet wird. Beispiele für *simple forms* sind: *you* **write** – *he* **sings** – *we* **study** *she* **went** – *they* **worked** Dabei sind **-s** und **-ed** keine Erweiterungen, sondern Endungen (*3rd person singular present* und *past tense*).	*Progressive* lässt sich mit <u>fortlaufend</u> oder <u>fortschreitend</u> übersetzen. Damit bezeichnen wir **Vorgänge**, die noch **nicht abgeschlossen** sind, die **noch andauern**. Die deutsche Bezeichnung für *progressive form* ist daher auch „Dauerform" oder „Verlaufsform". Neben *progressive form* werden auch noch die Bezeichnungen *continuous form* oder *expanded form* verwendet. Sie meinen alle das Gleiche.
Grundsätzliche Verwendung	
Simple form wird immer dann verwendet, wenn es um die **Handlung als solche** geht. Man erfährt durch *simple form* einfach, <u>was geschieht</u>, <u>geschah</u> oder <u>geschehen wird</u>. Das Subjekt tut etwas, tat etwas oder wird etwas tun. *You* **write** *letters every day.* *You* **wrote** *a letter an hour ago.* *You* **have written** *four letters today.*	*Progressive form* beschreibt den **Verlauf einer Handlung**. Man erfährt, <u>was</u> **zu einem bestimmten Zeitpunkt** <u>gerade geschieht</u>, <u>geschah</u> oder <u>geschehen wird</u>. Das Subjekt ist (war, ...) gerade dabei, etwas zu tun. *You* **are writing** *letters right now.* *You* **were writing** *letters when I ...* *You* **have been writing** *letters for ...*

Hier siehst du, wie *simple form* und *progressive form* **in den verschiedenen Zeitstufen** gebildet werden (über die Anwendung informierst du dich am besten in den „Spezialkapiteln" über die Zeitstufen). Als „Verb für alle Zwecke" nehmen wir **"to ask"**.

simple form	*progressive form*
present tense	
I, you, we, they **ask** he, she, it **ask<u>s</u>**	I **am** asking he, she, it **is** asking you, we, they **are** asking
present perfect tense	
I, you, we, they **have** asked he, she, it **has** asked	I, you, we, they **have been asking** he, she, it **has been** asking
past tense	
(all persons) **asked**	I, he, she, it **was** asking you, we, they **were** asking
past perfect tense	
(all persons) **had asked**	(all persons) **had been** asking
future with will	
(all persons) **will ask**	(all persons) **will be** asking

Über Bildung und Anwendung von **conditional present** und **conditional perfect** lernst du in Kapitel 4, Seite 30 **(Conditions)**. In diesen beiden „Zeitstufen" kommt *progressive form* so selten vor, dass wir uns hier nicht näher darum kümmern wollen.

Achtung! Es gibt mehrere Gruppen von **Verben**, die **nicht in *progressive form*** auftreten. Es sind dies vor allem Verben, die (Gefühls- oder Bewusstseins-) **Zustände** beschreiben und nicht Handlungen. Dazu zählen:

hate – like – love – need – prefer – want   (mögen oder nicht mögen)
believe – know – mean – remember – unterstand   (Vorgänge im Bewusstsein)
hear – see – smell – taste   (Sinneswahrnehmungen)

                 Progressi**v**e Form & **S**imple Form

20 *P*ronouns
Fürwörter/Pronomen

A Persönliches Fürwort

1. Das **persönliche Fürwort** oder *personal pronoun* ist ein **Ersatzwort**, meist für ein **Nomen** (Hauptwort). Ein paar Beispiele sollen das zeigen:

<u>This boy</u> has lots of toys.	→	**He** has lots of toys.
Do you like <u>my new skis</u>?	→	Do you like **them**?
<u>People</u> don't like <u>noise</u>.	→	**They** don't like **it**.

2. Das *personal pronoun* tritt entweder als **Subjekt** oder als **Objekt** auf. Und bei Joe, dem Obsthändler, sieht das dann so aus:

das *personal pronoun* als **Subjekt**		Person	das *personal pronoun* als **Objekt**
I	like green apples.	1st sing.	Joe gave **me** two apples.
You	like red apples.	2nd sing.	Joe gave **you** one apple.
He	like**s** oranges better.		Joe gave **him** an orange.
She	like**s** oranges, too.	3rd sing.	Joe gave **her** two oranges.
It	doesn't like oranges.		Joe didn't give **it** an orange.
We	like bananas.	1st plur.	Joe gave **us** some bananas.
You	like pineapples better.	2nd plur.	Joe gave **you** some pineapples.
They	like kiwis best.	3rd plur.	Joe gave **them** some kiwis.

Achtung bei *3rd person singular*!

> *he, she* und *it* entsprechen **nicht ganz** dem deutschen **er, sie** und **es**.
> *he* und *she* darfst du nur **für Personen** (und Haustiere) sagen;
> *it* steht **für Dinge** und (sonstige) **Tiere**.

Daher:	<u>Er</u> (der Tisch) hat vier Beine.	→	**It** has four legs.
	<u>Sie</u> (die Lampe) funktioniert nicht.	→	**It** doesn't work.
	<u>Es</u> (das Auto) schaut neu aus.	→	**It** looks new.
Aber:	<u>Es</u> (das Mädchen) lacht.	→	**She** is laughing.

20A Setze die passenden *personal pronouns* ein. In den ersten acht Sätzen musst du dich nur auf die Subjektgruppe konzentrieren.

1. Look, there's a spider in the corner! – Is … dead? I hate spiders.
2. Is Joe at home, Mrs Johnson? – Yes, Frank, … is in his room.
3. Look, there are Jill and John. I think … are very good friends.
4. My brother and I are in the same school, but … do not have the same teachers.
5. Do you like Elizabeth? – No, I don't. I think … is arrogant.
6. Thank you for the ice-cream, Mr Stevens. … was very good.
7. Is this your sweater, Frank? – No, sir, … have a blue sweater, not a green one.
8. Tom and Harry, can … answer my question? – No, sir, … can't!

In den folgenden Sätzen geht es um das *personal pronoun* als Objekt. Setze also wieder die passenden Fürwörter ein.

9. Arnie is hiding in the tree. Can you see … ?
10. Where are my glasses? I cannot find …
11. I don't like George very much. Please don't tell … my address.
12. Look, there is Mrs Masters. Let's ask … about the exam.
13. Why do you ask … ? I have no idea where Joe is.
14. The football is somewhere in the garden. Can you see … ?
15. Children, where are … ? Please shout "Here we are!".
16. We can't open this door! Can you help …, please?

In den letzten sechs Sätzen sind bestimmte Satzteile unterstrichen. Ersetze sie durch *personal pronouns* (als Subjekt oder als Objekt).

17. Please don't tell <u>Maria</u> about <u>our little talk</u>.
18. <u>Children</u> like <u>pizza</u>. <u>Pizza</u> is okay.
19. <u>Robert</u> is going to ask <u>his mother</u> for more pocket money.
20. <u>Fred and I</u> are waiting for <u>the girls</u>.
21. <u>Betty</u> has asked <u>the boys</u> to come to her party.
22. Ask <u>Jerry</u>! He knows <u>the answer</u>.

*P*r*onouns*

B Besitzanzeigendes Fürwort

Das **besitzanzeigende Fürwort** oder *possessive pronoun* zeigt an, **wem** oder **zu wem** etwas gehört. Es kommt **mit oder anstelle** eines **Nomens** vor. Das sieht dann so aus:

mit einem **Nomen**			Person	anstelle eines **Nomens**	
This is	**my**	snowboard.	1st sing.	It is	**mine**.
Is this	**your**	snowboard?	2nd sing.	Is it	**yours**?
This is	**his**	lift ticket.		It is	**his**.
This is	**her**	pullover.	3rd sing.	It is	**hers**.
This is	**its**	place.		(It is	**its**.)
These are	**our**	skis.	1st plur.	They are	**ours**.
Are they	**your**	skis?	2nd plur.	Are they	**yours**?
They are	**their**	skis.	3rd plur.	They are	**theirs**.

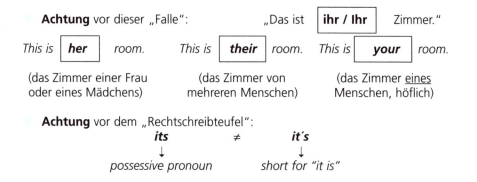

Achtung vor dieser „Falle": „Das ist **ihr / Ihr** Zimmer."

This is **her** room. | This is **their** room. | This is **your** room.

(das Zimmer einer Frau oder eines Mädchens) | (das Zimmer von mehreren Menschen) | (das Zimmer eines Menschen, höflich)

Achtung vor dem „Rechtschreibteufel":

its ≠ *it's*
↓   ↓
possessive pronoun   *short for "it is"*

C Hinweisendes Fürwort

Das **hinweisende Fürwort** oder *demonstrative pronoun* hebt eine **Person** (Personen) oder ein **Ding** (Dinge) aus einer Menge heraus, indem es auf sie „hinweist". Die wichtigsten *demonstrative pronouns* sind:

this	*these*	**der** (die, das); **dieser** (diese, dieses) **hier**
that	*those*	**der** (die, das); **dieser** (diese, dieses) **dort**
singular	*plural*	

this und *these*   bezeichnet das, was **näher** beim Sprecher liegt;
that und *those*   bezeichnet das, was **weiter weg** vom Sprecher liegt.

Bei diesen Wörtern hängt die Wortwahl sehr vom jeweiligen **Standpunkt** ab. Was für den einen *"this"* und *"these"* ist, ist für den anderen *"that"* und *"those"*.

Das **bezügliche Fürwort** oder *relative pronoun* wird in **Kapitel 22**, ab Seite 134 ausführlich besprochen.

Welches *possessive pronoun* passt? Schau dir die folgenden Situationen genau an und entscheide dich!

1. I like Angela and … sister, but I don´t like … brother. He´s a bully.
2. My dad is okay. He sometimes lets me ride … motorbike.
3. Mr Freeman says we have to do … homework at home and not here.
4. Joe, is this … pen? – No, … pen is blue, not grey.
5. Tim and Sally are my neighbours. I often go to … place to play video games.
6. The capital of Austria is Vienna. … German name is "Wien".
7. Elsie and Jane, show me … hands! They are dirty again!
8. Robert and Peter are my brothers. We live in a nice house together with … parents and … grandma.

Bei den nächsten Sätzen wird nach dem *possessive pronoun* <u>anstelle</u> eines Nomens gesucht. Schau dir die Angaben wieder genau an und entscheide dich.

Beispiel: *Is this Dominic´s folder?* → *Yes, it´s his. / No, it isn´t his.*

9. Is this Veronica´s picture album? –
   Yes, it´s …
10. David, is this your bus pass? –
    Let me see!, No, it isn´t …
11. Look, Tim, I have found a bunch of keys.
    You have lost …, haven´t you?
12. This looks like the children´s football! –
    Yes, it´s …
13. Bill and Bob, is this your car over there? –
    Yes, it´s …
14. These are your brother´s shoes, aren´t they? –
    Yes, I think they are …
15. Boys, look here! There are some clothes
    on the floor. I think they are …
16. Get off this bike! It´s …, not … !

Ein **Überblick** über die *personal* und *possessive pronouns* zum raschen Nachschlagen!

personal (subject)	possessive (with noun)	possessive (without noun)	personal (object)
I	*my*	*mine*	*me*
you	*your*	*yours*	*you*
he – she – it	*his – her – its*	*his – hers – its*	*him – her – it*
we	*our*	*ours*	*us*
you	*your*	*yours*	*you*
they	*their*	*theirs*	*them*

Pronouns

E Rückbezügliches Fürwort

1.

Das **rückbezügliche Fürwort** oder **reflexive pronoun** gleicht in vielem seinem deutschen Gegenstück, doch gibt es auch Unterschiede, die zu Fehlern verleiten können.

Die *reflexive pronouns* nennt man manchmal auch die **"self-pronouns"**.

singular					plural			
I	taught	**myself**	to ski.	1st	**We**	taught	**ourselves**	to ski.
You	taught	**yourself**	to ski.	2nd	**You**	taught	**yourselves**	to ski.
He	taught	**himself**	to ski.					
She	taught	**herself**	to ski.	3rd	**They**	taught	**themselves**	to ski.
(It	taught	**itself**	to ski.)					

Achte besonders auf diese drei Dinge!

- Es heißt **-self**, wenn du von einer **einzelnen Person** sprichst *(singular)* und **-selves**, wenn du von **mehreren Personen** sprichst *(plural)*.
- Es heißt daher **yourself** im *singular* und **yourselves** im *plural*.
- Es heißt **himself** und nicht *hisself*, **themselves** und nicht *theirselves*.

2.

Du verwendest das *reflexive pronoun* in den folgenden Situationen:

(a) Wenn man auf Deutsch sagt: **ich ... mich / mir; du ... dich / dir; er / sie ... sich; wir ... uns** und **ihr ... euch**.

> *I* often ask **myself** why I am so clever.
> (Ich frage mich oft, warum ich so klug bin!)

> *He* (Joe) fell and hurt **himself** badly.
> (Er stürzte und verletzte sich schwer.)

(b) Wenn man sagen will, dass jemand etwas **selbst** gemacht hat (daher auch die Bezeichnung **"self-pronouns"**).

> *Nobody helped Jane. **She** did it **herself**.*
> (Niemand hat Jane geholfen. Sie hat es selbst gemacht.)

> *Look, **we**'ve made those costumes **ourselves**!*
> (Wir haben diese Kostüme selbst gemacht!)

(c) Wenn man **eine Person oder ein Ding** besonders **hervorheben** will.

> *I heard the story from Joe. **He himself** told me everything.*
> (Ich habe ... von Joe gehört. Er selbst hat mir alles erzählt.)

> *After the storm, **the house itself** was okay, but the roof wasn't.*
> (... das Haus selbst war in Ordnung, aber das Dach nicht.)

20E Setze die passenden *reflexive pronouns* ein.

(a) „Ich ... mich, du ... dich, er ... sich, ...“

1. Fred, don't always look at ... in the mirror! We all know you look good!
2. Your cold will not cure *(heilen)* ... You'll have to see a doctor.
3. Olga's parents often ask ... what is the matter with their daughter.
4. Fritz was so angry that he could not control ... any more. He jumped up and ran out of the room.
5. Martina is very selfish. She thinks only of ..., never of others.
6. Boys, don't hurt ... with those knives!
7. Mum says I often talk to ... in my sleep.
8. When we come home from school, we often make ... a cold lunch.

(b) „selbst gemacht!“

9. Girls, did you make these dresses ... ? – Yes, and we are very proud!
10. You can't ask your brother for help, Jenny. You have to do your homework ...
11. When the Coopers go away on holiday, their children have to look after ... I think they are too young for this!
12. Did anyone tell you where the things were hidden? – No, I found it out ...
13. Ellen answered all the questions ... Nobody was there to help her.
14. Don't do it! Let Peter do it ... !
15. I hope they will soon build a computer that can program ...
16. We don't need a plumber *(Installateur)*. We can do it ...

(c) „Das gehört hervorgehoben!“

17. You play very well, Tony. I ... could not do it better.
18. The visit to the White House was fantastic. Unfortunately *(leider)* we did not see the President ...
19. How did you like "Fidelio"? – Well, the opera ... was okay, but the singers were terrible.
20. Don't worry about your cat, Mrs Jones. Martin and I ... will look after it *(sich kümmern um)* while you are in hospital.
21. Who told you about Joe and me? – You ..., don't you remember?
22. What are you doing in the Coopers' garden? – Playing hide-and-seek. But it's okay. The Coopers ... said we could come in and play.

Pronouns

(d) Wenn man sagen will, dass jemand **allein** war oder ist.

*Come and sit beside me! **I** don't like to be **by myself**.*
(Komm und setze dich zu mir. <u>Ich</u> bin nicht gern <u>allein</u>.)

*When I saw Claudia yesterday, **she** was sitting **by herself** in the park.*
(Als ich Claudia gestern sah, saß <u>sie alleine</u> im Park.)

(e) Man darf die *self-pronouns* **nicht mit "each other"** oder **"one another"** (einander, gegenseitig) **verwechseln**.

***Mac and Charlie** looked at **themselves** in the mirror and had a good laugh.*

***Mac and Charlie** looked at **each other (one another)** and had a good laugh.*

(f) Achtung, Unterschied! Es gibt Verben, die **im Deutschen mit** einem rückbezüglichen Fürwort verwendet werden, **im Englischen** aber **ohne** *reflexive pronoun* auskommen.

Ich kann es **mir** nicht leisten, zu verlieren.
I cannot <u>afford</u> to lose.

Wie fühlst **du dich**?
How do you <u>feel</u>?

Wir müssen **uns** beeilen!
We must <u>hurry</u>!

Sie treffen **sich** jeden Samstag.
They <u>meet</u> every Saturday.

Er kann **sich** nicht an das Datum erinnern.
He cannot <u>remember</u> the date.

Du wäschst **dir** nie die Hände vor dem Essen!
You never <u>wash</u> your hands before you eat.

Sie macht **sich** manchmal Sorgen um mich.
She sometimes <u>worries</u> about me.

(d) „allein"

1. What are you doing here by …, Mary?
2. On a Saturday evening, I hate to be by …
3. Young people under 14 are not allowed to stay out by … after midnight.
4. My grandpa lives by …, but he doesn´t like it.
5. Last summer, my sister and I went to the USA by … It was fantastic.
6. Do you want to be by …, girls, or I can sit with you?
7. I often see Carol play by … Doesn´t she have any friends?
8. The problem will not go away by … You´ll have to drive it away!

(e) „Vorsicht vor Verwechslungen!" Welche Möglichkeit stimmt? Bei einem Satz ist beides möglich!

9. Some people talk to *themselves / one another* in their sleep.
10. I met some people from Hungary in my last holiday. They did not speak English, I did not speak Hungarian, so we spoke German with *ourselves / one another.*
11. Willie and I put on our clown costumes and looked at *ourselves / each other*. Then we had a good laugh because we looked so funny.
12. Mary and Mollie are good friends, but sometimes they do not like *themselves / each other* very much.

(f) „Achtung, Unterschied!" Übersetze die folgenden Sätze ins Englische. Aber Vorsicht, ein paar Mal wirst du das *reflexive pronoun* schon brauchen!

13. Ich kann mich nicht an deinen Namen erinnern.
14. Geh und wasch dir das Gesicht!
15. Du musst dich beeilen!
16. Angie fühlt sich nicht wohl.
17. Charlie denkt immer nur an sich.
18. Wir treffen uns jeden Tag nach der Schule.
19. Kannst du dir das Moped wirklich leisten?
20. Ruf einen Arzt! Joe hat sich verletzt.
21. Du kannst mitkommen *(come with us)*, aber du musst dir alles selbst bezahlen.
22. Nach der Schule mache ich mir oft einen Sandwich.

Pronouns

21 Question & Negation
Frage und Verneinung

Jede Frage (mit Ausnahme der Frage nach dem Subjekt) **und jede Verneinung** muss **ein Hilfsverb** enthalten. Hilfszeitwörter sind Verben, die für sich allein keine Handlung ausdrücken. Sie treten daher gemeinsam mit einem Vollverb (Hauptzeitwort) auf.

The children	can must will	play	football.
The children	have	played	football
The children	are	playing	football.
	Hilfsverb	**Vollverb**	

 ## A Bildung der Entscheidungsfrage

Die **Entscheidungsfrage** (oder *general question*) dient als Ausgangspunkt für alle anderen Fragen. Sie heißt Entscheidungsfrage, weil man sich bei der Antwort zwischen „Ja" und „Nein" entscheiden muss.

Die Entscheidungsfrage **mit Hilfszeitwort** wird wie im Deutschen gebildet: das Hilfszeitwort wandert an die Spitze des Satzes:

Joe **is** your best friend.   We **can** go now.

Is Joe your best friend?   **Can** we go now?

 ## B Verneinung

Die **Verneinung mit Hilfsverb** funktioniert ebenso einfach: Nach das Hilfsverb schiebt sich das Wörtchen **"not"**.

Joe **is** your best friend. → Joe **is not** your best friend.
We **can** go now. → We **cannot** go now.

Allerdings – es gibt auch **Ausnahmen**! Sie betreffen *may* und *must*.

- We **may** see the film. → **Erlaubnis oder Möglichkeit**
  We **may not** see the film. → **mildes Verbot** („eher nicht")
  We **must not** see the film. → **strenges Verbot** („auf keinen Fall")

- You **must** leave the room. → **Gebot, Befehl** („du musst!")
  You **need not** leave the room. → **„du musst nicht, du brauchst nicht"**

Hilfszeitwörter sind:
alle Formen von *be*
alle Formen von *have*
can – could
may, must, shall
will – would

und manchmal:
do – does – did

21A

Bilde von den folgenden Sätzen die Entscheidungsfrage und die Verneinung.

21B

1. Bill is at home.
2. You can come to my party. *(Bilde die Frage mit "I".)*
3. We are tired. *(Bilde die Frage mit "you".)*
4. Joe has got fifty stickers.
5. I am late.
6. Joe must go now.
7. The boys may watch TV.
8. The girls have got enough money.

Die gleiche Übung, mit anderen Hilfsverben.

9. We could get into the museum. *(Bilde die Frage mit "you".)*
10. They will show "Star Trek VII" next week.
11. I have found my socks. *(Bilde die Frage mit "you".)*
12. The presents were in the boxes.
13. You should talk to Martin and Jane.
14. Ralph may read this letter.
15. It has snowed all night.
16. Dad is going to repair my bike.
17. We must do exercises 5 to 12.
18. Harry will show you the way.
19. Vera has finished her homework.
20. You may (can) stay out until 11.
21. Frank can walk on his hands.
22. We must be there before 8 o´clock.

Question & Negation

1. Die **Ergänzungsfrage** lässt sich leicht von der Entscheidungsfrage ableiten. Eine Ergänzungsfrage zielt auf einen bestimmten Satzteil ab und wird **immer** von einem **Fragewort** eingeleitet.

Joe	**is**	_in his room_	_in the afternoon_.	

	Is	Joe	in his room	in the afternoon?	→	general qu.
Where	is	Joe	——	in the afternoon?	→	place
When	is	Joe	in his room?	——	→	time
Who	is	——	in his room	in the afternoon?	→	subject

The girls	**have**	got	_new dresses_.	

	Have	the girls	got	new dresses?	→	general qu.
What	have	the girls	got?	——	→	object
Who	**has**	——	got	new dresses?	→	subject

Achtung! Die **Subjektfrage** verlangt **_3rd person singular_**.
Das heißt, _"who "_ verhält sich so wie _"he – she – it"_.

The children **are** tired.	→	_Who_ **is** tired?
Mum and Dad **were** in town.	→	_Who_ **was** in town?
_We_ **have** seen the film.	→	_Who_ **has** seen the film?

2. Die **Fragewörter** für die Ergänzungsfragen sind:

who?	→	Subjekt	Who is this man?	(wer?)
who(m)?	→	Objekt	Who(m) shall we ask?	(wem? wen?)
whose?	→	Besitz	Whose CD is this?	(wessen?)
what?	→	Objekt	What have you got here?	(was?)
	→	Subjekt	What is in this box?	(was?)
where?	→	Ort	Where are the children?	(wo?)
when?	→	Zeit	When is school over?	(wann?)
why?	→	Grund	Why are you here?	(warum?)
how?	→	Art und Weise	How was the exam?	(wie?)

21C Bilde die Entscheidungsfrage und die Verneinung. Stelle auch möglichst viele Ergänzungsfragen.

1. Bill's father has got a new job.
2. The boys can play football after lunch.
3. Marion is in the swimming club.
4. My friends are playing rave music.
5. You must read this letter. *(Bilde die Fragen mit "I".)*
6. The children were in the cinema.
7. Lydia was in hospital.
8. Lukas can eat three Big Macs.

Weiter so! Aber – jetzt auch mit *"whose?"* und *"why?"*

9. This was Tina's house some years ago.
10. We can use my parents' VCR.
11. Joe is riding Bill's bike today.
12. You will sleep in Angie's room tonight.
13. Henry has gone home because he is tired.
14. Mum and Dad were in the hospital to visit Grandma.
15. You must learn these words because they are important. *(Bilde ... mit "I".)*
16. The children could buy the models because they were cheap.

Und noch ein Durchgang, dieses Mal auch mit *"how?"* und *"who(m)?"*

17. Dinner was very expensive.
18. We must walk faster because it is late.
19. Sonja can play the piano well.
20. You must ask Uncle Joe. *(Bilde die Fragen mit "I".)*
21. We have seen the boys at the tennis court. *(Bilde die Fragen mit "you".)*
22. Daisy and Nora are going to visit us tomorrow.
23. You can interview Mr Black next week. *(Bilde die Fragen mit "I".)*
24. Judy will marry Sam one day.

Question & Negation

3. Wenn in einem Satz **kein Hilfsverb** vorkommt, dann bildet man Frage und Verneinung …

- in **present tense** mit **do (not)** oder **does (not)** *(3rd person singular)*;
- in **past tense** mit **did (not)**.
- **Do, does** und **did** werden damit zu **Hilfsverben**. Sie treten immer **gemeinsam mit** einem **Vollverb** auf. Dieses Vollverb steht immer in **base form** (Infinitiv, 1. Stammform).

D Entscheidungsfrage und Verneinung mit *"do – does – did"*

Beginnen wir mit der **Entscheidungsfrage** und der **Verneinung**, denn sie sind die Ausgangspunkte für die Ergänzungsfragen:

Do	We		**write**	*letters at school.*
	we		**write**	*letters at school?*
	We	**do not**	**write**	*letters at school.*

keine Veränderungen des Vollverbs bei **do**

Does	Joe		**writes**	*letters at home.*
	Joe		**write**	*letters at home?*
	Joe	**does not**	**write**	*letters at home.*

3rd person -s wandert vom Vollverb zu **does**

Did	Tim		**wrote**	*a letter last week.*
	Tim		**write**	*a letter last week?*
	Tim	**did not**	**write**	*a letter last week.*

past tense wandert vom Vollverb zu **did**

E Ergänzungsfragen mit *"do – does – did"*

Die **Ergänzungsfragen** lassen sich mit Hilfe der Entscheidungsfrage leicht bilden. Du stellst die **Fragewörter** einfach **vor do, does** oder **did**.
Im Übrigen gelten dieselben „Gesetze" wie für die Entscheidungsfrage.

Jeremy plays football in the park every afternoon because he likes it .

	Does	Jeremy	play football	in the park	every afternoon?	
What	**does**	Jeremy	play	——	in the park	every afternoon?
Where	**does**	Jeremy	play	football	——	every afternoon?
When	**does**	Jeremy	play	football	in the park?	——
Why	**does**	Jeremy	play	football	in the park	every afternoon?

Achtung vor der **Subjektfrage!** Sie verlangt wieder **3rd person singular**. Das spielt aber nur in *present tense* eine Rolle, da in *past tense* sowieso alle Personen gleich sind.	**Achtung** vor der **Objektfrage mit who!** Sie verlangt – im Gegensatz zur Subjektfrage – die **Umschreibung mit do, does** oder **did.**
The children **play** *football.* → *Who* **plays** *football?*	*Who told you the story? – Joe!* *Who(m)* **did** *Joe* **tell** *the story? – Me!*

21D Bilde von den folgenden Sätzen die Entscheidungsfrage und die Verneinung.

1. Dad works in an office in town.
2. Before that he went to university.
3. Mum and Dad met at university.
4. They travelled to all corners of the world together.
5. Then they bought a nice little house.
6. Grandma and Grandpa live with us.
7. Grandma cooks for us every day.
8. We often play cards together.
9. I always win those card games.
10. Grandpa sometimes lets me win.

21E Bilde die Entscheidungsfrage und die Verneinung und stelle so viele Ergänzungsfragen, wie du kannst. Verwende alle geeigneten Fragewörter.

1. My little brother wants to watch videos every afternoon.
2. Every morning, George and Steve do their homework on the train.
3. My dad reads three newspapers every day because he likes reading.
4. My friends sang beautifully at my birthday party.
5. Somebody stole our neighbour's lawnmower *(Rasenmäher)* last night.
6. In our summer holiday we stayed at a very nice hotel.
7. Greg bought a moped last week because his grandmother gave him the money.
8. Bianca and Tania take dancing lessons after school.

Bilde von den folgenden Sätzen nur die Frage nach dem Subjekt und nach den Objekten. Achte bei der Objektfrage auf das Fragewort (*"what"* für Dinge, *"who"* für Personen).

9. Jimmy plays tennis in summer and in winter.
10. Our neighbours showed me their new car.
11. Herbert and Susie invite us to their Christmas party every year.
12. Markus gave Sandra a kiss.

Question & Negation

F „Nicht wahr?"-Frage

1. Eine englische Eigenheit ist die **„Nicht wahr?"-Frage**. Im Deutschen hängt man sie einheitlich an den Satz (die Aussage) an, wenn man sich nicht ganz sicher ist. Im Englischen ist das nicht so einfach. Es gibt zwar auch ein „Frageanhängsel" – auf Englisch **"question tag"** (manchmal auch *"tag question"*) – doch sieht es von Fall zu Fall verschieden aus:

Du bist müde, nicht wahr?	→	*You **are** tired, **aren´t** you?*
Bob ist Amerikaner, nicht wahr?	→	*Bob **is** American, **isn´t** he?*
Du wirst (doch) kommen, nicht wahr?	→	*You **will** come, **won´t** you?*
Joe studiert Mathe, nicht wahr?	→	*Joe **studies** maths, **doesn´t** he?*
Tom mag uns nicht, nicht wahr?	→	*Tom **doesn´t** like us, **does** he?*
Es gab viel zu essen, nicht wahr?	→	*There **was** a lot to eat, **wasn´t** there?*

2. Das sind die drei **„Hauptregeln"**, die sich daraus ableiten lassen:

Wenn die **Aussage** ein **Hilfsverb** enthält, wird es im Frageanhängsel *(question tag)* **weiterverwendet**.

Wenn die Aussage nur ein **Vollverb** (Hauptzeitwort) enthält, wird im Frageanhängsel **do / don´t, does / doesn´t** oder **did / didn´t** verwendet.

Wenn die **Aussage positiv** (also nicht verneint) ist, wird das **Anhängsel verneint**.
Wenn die **Aussage negativ** (also verneint) ist, wird das **Anhängsel positiv** (also bejahend).

3. Daneben gibt es aber noch ein paar **„Nebenregeln"** zu beachten:

Aussage und Anhängsel stehen in **derselben Zeitstufe**.
Das **Subjekt der Aussage** wird durch das passende **persönliche Fürwort** im Anhängsel **ersetzt**.
Das „Scheinsubjekt" **"there"** (wie z.B. in *there is, there are, ...*) wird **weiterverwendet**.

4. **„Ausnahmen"** gibt es natürlich auch:

Man sagt: *I´m not late, am I?* Aber es heißt: *I **am** late, **aren´t** I?*
Nach der Aufforderung **"Let´s (go)!"** sagt man **"..., shall we?"**
Nach der Befehlsform **"Hold (this)!"** sagt man **"..., will you?"**

Wenn man auf diese Art fragt, erhält man meist die **Kurzantwort**.

You are tired, aren´t you?	→	*Yes, **I am**. / No, **I´m not**.*
Joe studies maths, doesn´t he?	→	*Yes, **he does**. / No, **he doesn´t**.*
There was ...., wasn´t there?	→	*Yes, **there was**. / No, **there wasn´t**.*

21F

Du bist dir deiner Sache nicht ganz sicher und möchtest dich vergewissern. Bilde mit den folgenden Sätzen die *question tag* und beantworte sie in Form von Kurzantworten.

1. Joe is a nice fellow, ... ? – Yes, ...
2. Mary isn't ill, ... ? – No, ...
3. Tell me, boys, you have hidden my trousers, ... ? – No, ...
4. Bill hasn't called yet, ... ? – Yes, ... / No, ...
5. The girls were late again, ... ? – No, ...
6. The weather was awful, ... ? – Yes, ...
7. The Millers are going away tomorrow, ... ? – Yes, ...
8. You won't tell my parents, ... ? – No, ... Don't worry.

Weiter geht es, aber mit etwas schwierigeren Beispielen.

9. Your dad works in an office, ... ? – No, ... He's a teacher.
10. You like Jenny, ... ? – Yes, I ... I think she's wonderful.
11. But Jenny doesn't like you, ... ? – Oh yes, ... !
12. There was someone at the door, ... ? – No, ... It was the wind.
13. Bob will be there too, ... ? – Yes, ... And Joe and Bill, too.
14. There isn't any orange juice left, ... ? – No, ... But there's some milk.
15. Carol doesn't live here any more, ... ? – No, ... She's moved away.
16. You won £ 1,500 in the lottery, ... ? – Yes, ... I couldn't believe it!

Zum Abschluss die höchste Schwierigkeitsstufe, mit allen „Ausnahmen".

17. I am not too loud, ... ? – No, ... / Yes, ...
18. Tony, let's call Jerry , ... ? – Yes, let's. He's fun.
19. Open the window, ... ? It's too hot in here.
20. Pass me the sugar, ... ? – Here you are! – Thanks.
21. You weren't invited to Sally's party, ... ? – Oh yes, ... , but I couldn't come. Victor was there, too, ... ? – No, ... He was ill that day.
22. Put the things on the table, ... ? I'll put them away later.
23. I am your friend, ... ? – Yes, ... Your are okay.
24. In New Zealand, there are no snakes, ... ? – No, ... –
    Let's go there, ... ?

Question & Negation

22 RelatiVe Clauses
Relativsätze

Relativsätze sind Gliedsätze, die Bezüge zwischen einzelnen Teilen des Satzes herstellen und erklären. Relativsätze werden immer von bezüglichen Fürwörtern oder **Relativpronomen** eingeleitet. *Relative pronouns* sind Fürwörter, die sich **auf etwas vorher Genanntes beziehen**. Sie stehen immer sofort nach diesem Bezugswort.

Die *relative pronouns* sind:

> **who – which – that – (whom) – whose – what – where – why**

 ### Relativpronomen bei Personen

Wenn sich der Relativsatz auf eine **Person** bezieht, dann kommen folgende *relative pronouns* in Frage:

who (that)   Wenn das Bezugswort das **Subjekt** des Satzes ist, zieht man *"who"* vor; *"that"* ist aber ebenfalls möglich.

> *The boy **who (that)** sits next to me in class is my best friend.*
> → Der Bub, der neben mir sitzt, ...

whose   *"whose"* vertritt den Genitiv (2. Fall) und drückt ein **Besitzverhältnis** oder eine **Zugehörigkeit** aus.

> *The boy **whose** bike I am riding is my best friend.*
> → Der Bub, dessen Rad ich fahre, ...

who(m) that   Wenn das Bezugswort das **Objekt** ist, verwendet man heute meist *"who"* oder *"that"* oder man lässt das *relative pronoun* ganz weg (siehe auch Abschnitt **22G**, Seite 138). *"Whom"* ist eine ältere Form, die heute seltener verwendet wird.

> *The boy **who / that** you will meet tonight is my best friend.*
> *The boy you will meet tonight ...*
> *The boy whom you will meet tonight ...*
> → Der Bub, den du heute Abend treffen wirst, ...

22A Verwende *who* und *whose* (und statt *whom* auch besser *who* oder *that*) in den folgenden Sätzen. Setze das passende *relative pronoun* ein.

1. Boys and girls ... want to see "Hercules" today please contact Mr Ramsey.
2. The people ... we are visiting tonight are from Australia.
3. Do you like people ... know everything better? I hate them.

4. This is the boy ... bike was stolen. He wants to speak with the police.
5. Did you know the girl ... we just saw in the park? That was Isabella!
6. I don't know the people ... you are talking about. What's their name?
7. Where's the boy ... was sitting here a minute ago? I must ask him something.

8. Look, there are the Wilsons. That's the family ... house was damaged by the tornado last year.
9. Does anybody know the people ... car is parked outside the house? They have left the lights on.
10. Are you the person ... said I broke Mrs Johnson's window? You know it's not true!
11. What do you think of the two Americans ... you met at my party last week? I think they are very nice.

12. The lady ... we are going to visit is my father's aunt. She is very rich.
13. I would like to speak with the person ... has sent me this note.
14. Are you the man ... picture was on TV? I am sure it was you!
15. Don't trust *(vertrauen)* people ... don't look you in the eye when they speak with you.
16. "Hansel and Gretel" is about two children ... parents leave them alone in the woods.

RelatiVe Clauses

B   Relativpronomen bei Sachen

Wenn sich der Relativsatz auf eine **Sache** bezieht, dann kommen folgende *relative pronouns* in Frage:

that Wenn das Bezugswort das **Subjekt** des Satzes ist, zieht man
which *"that"* vor; *"which"* ist aber ebenfalls möglich.

> <u>Books</u> **that / which** *do not have any pictures are boring.*
> → <u>Bücher, die</u> keine Bilder aufweisen, ...

> Wenn das Bezugswort das **Objekt** ist, verwendet man heute
> meist **"that"** oder man lässt das *relative pronoun* ganz weg
> (siehe auch Abschnitt **22G**, Seite 138).

> <u>The books</u> **(that / which)** *we bought yesterday have dirty and torn
> pages.*
> → <u>Die Bücher, die</u> wir gestern kauften, ...

whose *"whose"* vertritt den Genitiv (2. Fall) und drückt ein
Besitzverhältnis oder eine **Zugehörigkeit** aus.

> <u>Books</u> **whose** *pages are dirty and torn* (zerrissen) *cannot be sold.*
> → <u>Bücher, deren</u> Seiten verschmutzt ... sind, ...

C   "that"

Das Relativpronomen **"that"** ist ein besonderer Fall. Es kann sich **auf Personen**
ebenso beziehen **wie auf Sachen**, und es gibt Fälle, in denen man *"that"*
verwenden soll:

- wenn das „Bezugswort" aus **Personen und Nicht-Personen zugleich**
  besteht (kommt sehr selten vor).
  > *Let's take a picture of* <u>the farmer and his horse</u> **that** *are working
  > there.*

- wenn das „Bezugswort" einen **Superlativ** (the best, the ugliest, ...) oder
  ein **„Extremwort"** (the first, the only, ...) enthält.
  > *You are the* <u>only person</u> **that** *can help us now.*
  > *The "Dusenberg Excalibur" is the* <u>most expensive car</u> **that** *is produced
  > at the moment.*

D   "which"

Wenn sich ein Relativsatz auf den **gesamten vorherigen Satz** bezieht, wird
"which" als *relative pronoun* eingesetzt. Vor *"which"* steht dann ein **Komma**.

> <u>Grandma sent me £ 50 for my birthday</u>. *I liked* <u>that</u> *very much.*
> *Grandma sent me £ 50,* **which** *I liked very much.*

22B

22C

Setze das passende *relative pronoun* ein.

1. Hansel and Gretel came to a house ... walls were made of gingerbread.
2. My friend had a cat ... had only three legs, but he loved it.
3. The street ... leads to our house is not easy to find.
4. Hermann was the first boy from our town ... won a medal.
5. New York is sometimes called "the city ... never sleeps".
6. New York is a city ... taxis are very famous.
7. New York is a place ... I would like to visit one day.
8. In Scotland we visited a castle ... walls were 12 m thick.
9. Look at the boy and his dog ... are playing over there! Don't they look lovely?
10. The roses ... Mum got yesterday still look fresh.
11. Did you get the letter ... I sent you last week?
12. I'm so happy! I passed my English exam. That's the best thing ... could happen to me!

22D

Verbinde die folgenden Sätze mit Hilfe von *"which"*. Vergiss dabei nicht auf das Komma!

1. We spent our skiing holiday in Switzerland. This was cheaper than we had thought.
2. Sometimes our maths teacher gets mad at us. This is not very funny.
3. I could answer all the questions on the test paper. This was a great surprise for everyone.
4. Stanley tells everybody that I've taken his new pen. But this is not true.
5. Joe found a summer job at the swimming pool. This is what he wanted.
6. Our team lost the match. This did not surprise anybody.
7. We had to run 10 laps *(Runden)* around the football field today. This made us very tired.
8. Max has asked me to go to the dance with him. This is wonderful.

22A-D

Versuche, die folgenden Satzpaare mit Hilfe von *relative pronouns* miteinander zu verbinden.

Beispiel: *I don't know this man. He is watching us.*
            I don't know **the man who** *is watching us.*

1. Yesterday we got a postcard. It had no stamp on it.
2. I've just talked to a boy. He knows Julia's telephone number.
3. Do you know the people? We are their guests tonight.
4. This morning Dad had to walk to work. This did not make him happy.
5. That coat belongs to my dad. I am wearing it at the moment.
6. Charlie works in a factory. It produces all kinds of paint.

Relati**V**e **C**lauses

E **"what"**

Das Relativpronomen **"what"** bezieht sich auf die Handlung. Diese wird durch das Prädikat – also das Verb – ausgedrückt. Vor *"what"* steht **kein Komma**.

> Does anybody <u>know</u> **what** we can do this afternoon?
> Go and <u>ask</u> Mum **what** she wants from the shop.
> Speak up! I can´t <u>hear</u> **what** you are saying.

F **"where"**

Wenn das „Bezugswort" ein **Ort** ist , verwenden wir **"where"** als Relativpronomen. Wenn wir sagen, warum etwas geschieht oder geschehen ist – wenn wir also den **Grund** *(reason)* angeben –, verwenden wir **"why"**.

> I love <u>the town</u> **where** I was born.
> <u>The reason</u> **why** I am late is because I missed the bus.

G **contact clauses**

Unter bestimmten Umständen kommen wir **ohne Relativpronomen** aus.
Wir nennen solche Sätze **contact clauses**, weil der Relativsatz dabei unmittelbar mit dem „Bezugswort" in Kontakt tritt.
Contact clauses sind immer dann möglich, wenn sich der Relativsatz auf das **Objekt** im Satz bezieht. Du erkennst das sehr leicht daran, dass auf das Relativpronomen *(who, that, ...)* **kein Verb** folgt. In diesen Fällen kann man das Fürwort weglassen.

> The people **who** we had invited did not come.
> The people • we had invited did not come.
> Where are the posters **that** I gave you last week?
> Where are the posters • I gave you last week?

> <u>These jeans</u> are too small. I bought <u>them</u> yesterday.
> The jeans **that** I bought yesterday are too small.
> The jeans • I bought yesterday are too small.

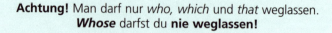

Achtung! Man darf nur *who, which* und *that* weglassen.
Whose darfst du **nie weglassen!**

Relative Clauses

22E Setze ein: *"which"* (mit Komma, bezieht sich auf den ganzen Satz) oder *"what"* (kein Komma, bezieht sich auf das Verb)?

1. Mr Smith left his house late at night ... is unusual.
2. Bob, can you tell me ... this word means in German?
3. Did you understand ... the speaker said?
4. Lots of people drink and drive ... is very dangerous.
5. Joe has got more than 100 CDs ... more than I have.
6. Fred wants to know ... we think of the new motorway.

22F Verbinde die folgenden Sätze mit *"where"*.
Beispiel: *This is the place. I lived here as a child.*
This is the place where *I lived as a child.*

1. The hotel was not very expensive. We stayed there in our holiday.
2. My grandpa showed us the town. He was born there.
3. This place is wonderful. My friends live here. *(The place ...)*
4. You can take the ring back to the shop. I bought it there.
5. Do you know a good restaurant? We could meet there.
6. This is the theatre! We saw "Miss Saigon" there.

22G *Relative pronoun* oder *contact clause*? Setze das Fürwort dort ein, wo es sein muss und lasse es dort weg, wo es möglich ist.

1. The person ... I like best in my class is Molly. She is really nice.
2. Are you the electrician? I am the one ... called you. We have no electricity in the house.
3. The documentary was about the man ... first climbed Mt. Everest. His name is Sir Edmund Hillary and he is from New Zealand.
4. A dictionary is the book ... you need if you want to find out the meaning of a word.
5. The film ... we saw last weekend was horrible and the actors were horrible, too.
6. The tunnel ... they are planning under the mountain is very expensive.

Verbinde die folgenden Sätze und bilde *contact clauses*. Das heißt, du darfst keine *relative pronouns* verwenden.

7. What did you do with the money? Your parents gave it to you last week.
8. The girls didn't tell us their names. We met them at the disco yesterday.
9. "Dr Jekyll and Mr Hyde" and "The Time Machine" are among the best books. I have read them.
10. Please bring me the letter. I have put it on my desk.
11. The new house looks very nice. Kevin and Flora have just bought it.
12. Have you still got the book? You borrowed it from me before Christmas.

Relative Clauses

Einschränkender und erweiternder Relativsatz

Ein Relativsatz kann für das Verstehen des Satzes unbedingt erforderlich sein, oder er kann uns „nur" zusätzliche Informationen liefern, die wir aber gar nicht wirklich brauchen würden.

Where is the book?
The girl is here again.
This is the man.

→ Wenn wir diese Sätze so stehen lassen, weiß niemand, welches Buch, welches Mädchen oder welchen Mann wir meinen.
Wir müssen daher schon etwas genauer werden.

*Where is the book **(that)** you borrowed from me last week?*
*The girl **whose** mother you met yesterday is here again.*
*This is the man **who** has shown us the way.*

→ Jetzt ist alles klar. Wir wissen, wer gemeint ist. Die Relativsätze haben die große Zahl der Möglichkeiten auf eine eingeschränkt.

> Ein Relativsatz, der die Zahl der Möglichkeiten auf einen bestimmten Fall einschränkt, heißt **einschränkender Relativsatz**. Er ist **für das Verstehen** des Satzes **erforderlich**.

Für den einschränkenden Relativsatz – auf Englisch *defining relative clause* – gelten folgende „Regeln":
- Er wird **ohne Kommas** direkt nach das Bezugswort gestellt;
- das *relative pronoun* kann **wegfallen**, wenn sich der Relativsatz auf das **Objekt** des Satzes bezieht.

Where is "The Name of the Rose"?
Brigid Jones is here again.
This is Joe Cooper.

→ Diese Sätze sind völlig klar; wir wissen ganz genau, wer oder was gemeint ist. Wir brauchen keine weitere Erklärung oder Einschränkung.

*Where is "The Name of the Rose" **, which** you borrowed ... last week?*
*Brigid Jones **, whose** mother you met yesterday **,** is here again.*
*This is Joe Cooper **, who** has shown us the way.*

→ Der Relativsatz liefert uns „bloß" zusätzliche (oder erweiternde) Informationen, die wie für das Verstehen des Satzes nicht unbedingt brauchen.

> Ein Relativsatz, der zusätzliche Informationen bietet, heißt **erweiternder Relativsatz**. Er ist **für das Verstehen** des Satzes **nicht erforderlich**.

Für den erweiternden Relativsatz – auf Englisch *non-defining relative clause* – gelten folgende „Regeln":

- Er wird **mit Kommas** vom Hauptsatz getrennt;
- das *relative pronoun* darf **auf keinen Fall wegfallen**;
- das *relative pronoun "that"* darf in einem erweiternden Relativsatz **nicht vorkommen**; für Personen wird *"who"* verwendet, für Sachen *"which"*.

Relative Clauses

22H „Einschränkend" oder „erweiternd"? Kommas oder keine Kommas?
Schau dir die Sätze genau an und entscheide.

1. This is the woman ... cooked the fantastic dinner last night.
2. Mrs Jones ... cooked the fantastic dinner last night is my mother's best friend.
3. The Thames ... flows through London is quite clean again.
4. The river ... flows through London is called the Thames.
5. Stockholm ... I have visited many times is the capital of Sweden.
6. What is the name of the town ... you visited last summer?
7. The songs of the Beatles ... were written in the 60s are still played today.
8. The Beatles song ... we like best is "Hey Jude".

Etwas Anspruchsvolleres: Verknüpfe die Sätze durch Relativsätze.

9. I often visit my friends in Westfield. (Westfield is 20 miles from New York.)
10. The sun was very hot that day. (The sun was standing directly above us.)
11. A woman told me that you were not there. (The woman opened the door.)
12. The police have found the girl. (The girl had been missing for two days.)
13. The school is famous for its football team. (My dad teaches there.)
14. General Grant was the 18th President of the United States. (His monument stands near the Hudson River in New York.)
15. Who are these children? (They are playing in front of your house.)
16. The Battle of Hastings changed the history of Britain. (It was fought in 1066.)
17. I haven't got a driving licence. (This means I am not allowed to drive.)
18. The hurricane caused *(verursachte)* a lot of damage. (The hurricane hit Florida in the spring of 1998.)
19. Hurricane "Andrew" caused a lot of damage. (The hurricane hit Florida in the summer of 1992.)
20. Relative clauses are easy to understand. (Relative clauses are an important point of English grammar.)

Relative Clauses

23 Singular & Plural
Einzahl und Mehrzahl

Das Problem „Einzahl und Mehrzahl" betrifft das **Hauptwort** (Nomen, **noun**).

A | Bildung der regelmäßigen Mehrzahl

1. Die **regelmäßige Mehrzahl** *(regular plural)* bildest du, indem du an das Hauptwort **-s** anhängst. Wenn das Wort mit einem Zischlaut endet, hängst du **-es** an und sprichst [-iz]. Zischlaute sind [s, z, ʃ, ʧ, ʤ, ks].

plural with **-s**		*plural* with **-es**	
apple → apple**s**	town → town**s**	bus → bus**es**	dish → dish**es**
desk → desk**s**	lamp → lamp**s**	watch → watch**es**	box → box**es**

2. Beim Anhängen von -s oder -es musst du allerdings die **Rechtschreibung** beachten:

Konsonant + y → -ies		-f(e) → -ves		Konsonant + o → -oes	
city	→ cit**ies**	wolf → wol**ves**		potato	→ potat**oes**
baby	→ bab**ies**	leaf → lea**ves**		tomato	→ tomat**oes**
cry	→ cr**ies**	life → li**ves**		motto	→ mott**o(e)s**

Achtung! Gilt nicht für alle Wörter!
z.B. roof → roof**s**   ghetto → ghet**tos**

B | Bildung der unregelmäßigen Mehrzahl

Nicht alle Hauptwörter bilden die Mehrzahl mit -*(e)s*. In diesem Fall sprechen wir von der **unregelmäßigen Mehrzahl**. Zu dieser Gruppe gehören nicht sehr viele Wörter; hier findest du eine Liste der Nomen, die du auf jeden Fall kennen solltest:

man → **men**	tooth → **teeth**	mouse → **mice**
woman → **women**	foot → **feet**	sheep → **sheep**
child → **children**	goose → **geese**	fish → **fish**

Setze die folgenden Sätze in die Mehrzahl. Achte dabei besonders auf das unter-
strichene Wort.

1. London is a large <u>city</u>. – *London and Los Angeles ...*
2. Greg is <u>a boy</u> from my class. – *Greg and Steven ...*
3. <u>A dog</u> can run fast.
4. Sometimes <u>the English class</u> is fun.
5. I need <u>a potato</u> and <u>a tomato</u> for the salad.
6. <u>The glass</u> is empty.
7. <u>The bus leaves</u> from here every ten minutes.
8. <u>The lady</u> who lives next door is <u>a teacher</u>.

23B Bilde auch von diesen Sätzen die Mehrzahl. Achte wieder auf die unterstrichenen
Wörter.

1. The <u>man</u> works in my uncle's <u>factory</u>.
2. Grandma has lost her last <u>tooth</u>.
3. My <u>foot</u> hurts after the long walk.
4. The <u>policeman</u> helped the <u>child</u> across the street.
5. The <u>mouse</u> ate all the cheese.
6. The farmer had <u>a sheep</u> and <u>a cow</u>.
7. Do you know the <u>woman</u> over there?
8. The <u>goose</u> ran away and the <u>man</u> ran after <u>it</u>.

Singular & Plural

C | **Hauptwörter, die es nur im Plural gibt**

1. Es gibt **Hauptwörter**, die im Englischen **nur im Plural vorkommen**, während sie im Deutschen in der Einzahl stehen. **Auch das Verb** hat dann eine **Pluralform**. Wichtige Wörter aus dieser Gruppe sind:

> *glasses – jeans – pants – pyjamas – scissors – shorts – trousers*
> Brille   Jeans (Unter-)Hose Pyjama   Schere   (kurze) Hose (lange)

Diese Wörter kannst du auch mit *"a pair of ..."* verwenden:

> *I need stronger glasses.* → *I need **a** stronger **pair of glasses**.*

2. Dann gibt es **Hauptwörter, die auf -s enden**, aber **wie in der Einzahl verwendet** werden. Auch das **Verb** steht dann im **Singular**. Dazu gehören:

> *gymnastics – math(ematic)s – news – physics*
> Turnen   Mathematik   Nachricht(en) Physik

> *I hate mathematics, but physics **is** my favourite subject.*
> *This **was** really good news. – The news **is** on at 7:30 p.m.*

> **!** **Achtung!** Verwende *person* im Singular, aber *people* im Plural.

> *Joe Brown **is** a̱ nice person̲. → The Browns **are** nice people̱.*

D | **Hauptwörter ohne Mehrzahlbildung**

1. Es gibt viele **Hauptwörter, die überhaupt keine Mehrzahl haben**. Sie bezeichnen **Sachen**, die man **nicht zählen** kann. Das heißt, man kann nicht „ein Geld", „zwei Wasser" usw. sagen. Zu dieser Gruppe gehören etwa:

> *gold – iron – milk – money – music – water – time – ...*

2. Die Gruppe umfasst im Englischen aber auch Wörter, die **im Deutschen** schon **zählbar** sind, wie zum Beispiel:

> *advice – bread – furniture – information – work*
> Rat   Brot   Möbel   Information   Arbeit

Kannst du mir einen Rat geben?	→	*Can you give me **some** advice?*
Bitte ein Brot mit Marmelade!	→	***A piece of** bread with jam, please.*
Das war eine wichtige Information.	→	*This was **important information**.*

3. **Einige Wörter** sind je nach Verwendung **entweder zählbar oder unzählbar**.

*There's **a hair** in my salad!*	≠	*Gina has **long, dark hair**.*
*Give me **the paper**, please!*	≠	*Give me **some paper**, please!*
(= newspaper)		*(= Schreibmaterial)*

Singular & Plural

1. Die Verwendung von **"much / little"** und **"many / few"** hängt davon ab, ob etwas zählbar ist oder nicht.

much / little	many / few
heißt „**viel**" / „**wenig**" bei **nicht zählbaren** Sachen das nachfolgende **Hauptwort** steht immer im **Singular**	heißt „**viele**" / „**wenige**" bei **zählbaren** Sachen das nachfolgende **Hauptwort** steht immer im **Plural**

2. Verwende *"much"* und *"many"* vor allem in **Verneinung** und **Frage** (besonders *"How much?"* und *"How many?"*).

> *Were there **many** people at the concert?*
> *Hurry up! We haven't got **much** time left!*

3. Verwende *"much"* und *"many"* nach **too** und **so**, auch in Frage und Verneinung.

> *There were **too many** people at the concert.*
> *I'm sorry, I haven't got **so much** much money with me.*

4. Verwende **"a lot of"** oder **"lots of"** in „normalen" Aussagesätzen, vor allem statt *"much"*.

> *I've got **lots of** posters in my room.   (or: I've got **many** posters ...)*
> *Last year we had **a lot of** snow.   (≠ ... we had **much** snow.)*

5. Verwende **"not enough"** statt *"too few"*. Aber – **"too little"** ist okay.

> *I did **not** get **enough** points to pass the exam.*
> *(≠ I got too few points to pass the exam.)*
> *Half a litre of Coke was **too little** (or: not enough) for all of us.*

23E Setze *much, many, a lot of / lots of* ein (1 bis 8), *little / few* (9 bis 12).

1. Run, Peter, we haven't got ... time left!
2. I think Joe smokes too ... ! – Yes, and he drinks too ..., too!
3. ... people get seasick when they make a boat trip.
4. Alice has ... books in her library, but she doesn't have ... comics.
5. There isn't ... to do in the country, but there are ... things to see.
6. Valerie can't go out today because she has ... work to to for school.
7. Bill Gates has so ... money that he can't spend it all.
8. Did you buy ... souvenirs while you were on holiday?
9. The room was almost empty. There were very ... people there.
10. There has been very ... rain this year.
11. At the moment I have ... time for my hobbies. I'm too busy.
12. George has ... friends because he is so aggressive.

Auch die folgenden Wörter richten sich nach Einzahl und Mehrzahl:

all

* heißt **„alle"** und bezieht sich auf die <u>Gesamtmenge</u>;
  tritt mit dem **Hauptwort im Plural** auf:
    ***All dogs** like chasing cats.*
    ***All my friends** were at my birthday party.*

* heißt **„ganz"** und bezeichnet eine <u>Zeitdauer</u>;
  tritt mit dem **Hauptwort im Singular** auf:
    *I've worked **all day**; I'm tired. – Mr Smith lives here **all year**.*
    ... den ganzen Tag.   ... das ganze Jahr.

* als ***„all (of) the"*** bezieht es sich auf <u>alle aus einer bestimmten Menge</u>:
    ***All (of) the dogs in our street** bark when the moon is full.*
    *Mr Clark wants to speak with **all the boys in the class**.*

every und each

* ***„every"*** heißt **„jeder"** und bezieht sich auf die <u>Gesamtmenge</u>;
  tritt mit dem **Hauptwort im Singular** auf:
    ***Every dog** likes chasing cats.*
    *I have seen **every film** with Brad Pitt.*

* ***„each (of)"*** heißt **„jeder"** und bezieht sich auf eine <u>Teilmenge</u>:
    ***Each boy in my class** spoke with Mr Clark.*
    ***Each of the boys in my class** spoke with Mr Clark.*

some

* heißt **„einige"** aus einer <u>Gesamtmenge</u>; bezeichnet **zählbare** Sachen:
    *I like **some films** better than others.*

* heißt **„etwas"** von einer <u>Gesamtmenge</u>; bezeichnet **unzählbare** Sachen:
    *Can I have **some water**, please?*

* ***„some of ..."*** heißt „einige / etwas" aus einer <u>Teilmenge</u>:
    ***Some of the people in our town** have dogs.*
    *You can have **some of the water in the bottle**, but not all of it.*

none of

* heißt **„keiner"**, meist aus einer <u>Teilmenge</u>; **Hauptwort im Plural**:
    ***None of my friends** could answer the questions.*

23F Setze die passenden Wörter ein.

1. Greg and Lukas play tennis ... Wednesday. They play ... afternoon.
2. I have taken ... my medicine. I need a new bottle.
3. ... of the girls on the team have finished the race, but ... of the boys are still running.
4. ... people have never heard of "badminton". They don't know how it is played.
5. Not ... boys like football; ... prefer tennis or volleyball.
6. ... of my friends wanted to go to the cinema, so I stayed at home, too, and did ... of my homework for next week.
7. Look at this mess! ... the books are where they should be!
8. ... woman likes fashion magazines. – No, ... women find them boring.

9. ... jeans in this shop are now cheaper.
10. ... people like sports and ... don't.
11. It snowed ... day yesterday, so ... of the trains did not run.
12. Can I have ... milk, please? – I'm sorry, but ... the bottles in the fridge are empty. Do you want ... applejuice instead *(stattdessen)*?
13. The TV team interviewed ... of the people in our town, but not me.
14. ... day has 24 hours, and ... week has seven days.
15. Last week was terrible! We had tests on ... day of the week.
16. The quiz was very difficult, but Martin could answer ... the questions.

17. ... the rooms of our hotel had satellite TV and a telephone.
18. I was very sad when I saw the letters. ... them was for me!
19. The rain was no problem because ... us had boots and an umbrella.
20. Take everything! ... this is for you!
21. Are your guests from Australia? – No, ... them are from England and ... are from South Africa.
22. ... my brothers will come to my parents' silver wedding anniversary.
23. Thirty people wanted the job, so the manager interviewed ... them.
24. Did you paint ... these pictures yourself? – No, only ... them. My dad painted the others.

Singular & Plural

24 "Some & Any"

"some" und **"any"** bedeuten beide das Gleiche: „etwas" oder „einige". Du darfst sie aber nicht nach Lust und Laune verwenden, sondern du musst einige Punkte beachten!

Das Gleiche gilt für die Zusammensetzungen **something / anything**, **somebody / anybody**, **someone / anyone** und **somewhere / anywhere**.

A | some

Du verwendest **"some"** und die Zusammensetzungen mit *"some"* in den folgen-den Fällen:

⚬ in **Aussagesätzen ohne Verneinung:**

*There are **some** people at the door. I think they are Mormons.*
*I think there is **something** wrong with me. I don't feel well.*
*I lost my keys **somewhere** between here and the bus stop.*

⚬ in **Fragen**, bei denen man mit einer **positiven Antwort** rechnet:

*Can you lend me **some** money, Joe? You'll get it back tomorrow.*
*Did you give Mary **something** to drink? – Yes, a glass of milk.*

B | any

Du verwendest **"any"** und die Zusammensetzungen mit *"any"* in den folgenden Fällen:

⚬ in **Aussagesätzen mit Verneinung:**

*Mum, there are**n't any** oranges left. Can you get some?*
*Grandpa **never** asks **anybody / anyone** for help. He is too proud.*

⚬ in **Fragen**, bei denen **jede Antwort möglich** ist:

*Does **anybody** know **anything** about this place?*
*Is Joe **anywhere** around? I must speak with him!*

⚬ in **„if-Sätzen":**

*I will tell you if **anyone** wants to talk to you.*
*If Joe gets **any** information for us, he will let us know.*

⚬ in **Aussagesätzen**, wenn **any** „(jedes) beliebige" bedeutet:

*You can take **any** car you like. – Okay, I'll take the BMW!*

"Some & Any"

24A

Bilde die Entscheidungsfrage *(general question)* und die Verneinung *(negation)* mit den folgenden Sätzen.

24B

1. Bill wants some ice for his orange juice.
2. I know something about Joe. *(Bilde die Frage mit "you".)*
3. Veronica lives somewhere near here.
4. We have found somebody to repair our car. *(Bilde die Frage mit "you".)*
5. Mum needs some help with the cooking.
6. Helen met some interesting men in summer camp.
7. Daisy knows someone from Scotland.
8. I have heard something about Donald's latest adventures. *(... mit "you".)*

Setze *some* oder *any* oder andere passende Formen ein.

9. Hello! Is ... at home? I can't see ... !
10. Does ... mind if I open the window? – Yes! ... of us have a cold.
11. Would you like ... to drink, Joe? – No, thanks. I've just had ... juice.
12. The old man is sleeping ... under a bridge, I think. – That's because he hasn't got ... to go. He is homeless.
13. Can I have ... paper for my typewriter, please? – Sure! Take ... ! It's ... over there on the desk.
14. Have you seen ... of these films? – No, I haven't, but Sue has seen ... of them.
15. Would you like ... more tea? – Yes, please. And could I have ... cookies, too, please?
16. If ... asks for me, tell them I'm not at home.
17. You can take ... of these books if you want ...
18. Hey, mum, the fridge is empty! There isn't ... to eat in the house.
19. Tony, please bring me ... milk, eggs and flour from the shop. I want to bake ... cookies.
20. This morning I had ... tea and toast for breakfast. What did you have? – Nothing. I usually don't have ... for breakfast.
21. Did you hear ... ? I thought I heard ... !
22. If you see Judy ..., please tell her I have ... letters for her. ... left them here for her.
23. Can you show me ... of the sights of the city? – Of course! Is there ... special that you would like to go?
24. You've got ... lovely flowerpots in your garden, Sophie. – Do you like them? You can take ... pot you want. – Really? I could need ... pots for my window-sill *(Fensterbrett)*.
25. This is an easy exercise. ... can do it!
26. Do you have ... idea what Mac said to Maria? – No, but I'm sure it was ... stupid.

"Some & Any"

25 The Word Order
Die Wortstellung

Die „Grundformel" für die englische *word order* lautet:

A S A P O A

A Die „erste Regel" der *word order:*

- Das **Subjekt** steht immer **vor** dem **Prädikat**.
- Das **Objekt** steht immer **sofort nach** dem **Prädikat**.
- **Niemals** steht ein Wort **zwischen Prädikat und Objekt**.

Sonya	*plays*	*the piano.*
Joe	*has found*	*a wallet.*

B Die „zweite Regel" der *word order:*

- **Orts- und Zeitangaben** stehen für gewöhnlich **am Satzende**, und zwar in der Reihenfolge **Ort vor Zeit** *(place before time)*.
- Bei **zwei Zeitangaben** am Satzende steht die **genauere vor** der **allgemeineren**.
- Wenn man Ort und / oder Zeit des Geschehens **hervorheben** will, kann man die Angaben auch **an den Satzanfang** stellen.

	Sonya	*plays*	*the piano*	***in her room***	***every day***.
Every day	*Sonya*	*plays*	*the piano*	***in her room***.	

C Die „dritte Regel" der *word order:*

Das **Häufigkeitsadverb** *(adverb of frequency)* steht:

- **zwischen Subjekt und** einteiligem **Prädikat**;
- **nach dem ersten Prädikatsteil** bei mehrteiligem Prädikat;
- **nach** der Form von ***"to be"***.

Sonya		**often**	*plays*	*the piano in her room.*
Sonya	*has*	**often**	*played*	*the piano in her room.*
Sonya	*is*	**never**	*tired of playing the piano.*	

25A

25B

Bilde sinnvolle Sätze mit den vorhandenen Satzteilen. Überlege, ob du irgendetwas besonders hervorheben willst.

1. every morning – drinks – Dad – coffee – in the office
2. the shopping bag – you – can – on the table – put
3. to the sports club – go – Mike and Jane – every Friday – at 4 p.m.
4. in the garden – plants – our neighbour – every spring – new flowers
5. Paul – two – computers – has got – in his room
6. my pocket money – gives – me – Mum – every Friday
7. we – on Saturday – no – maths – have
8. his sister – "Monopoly" – is – Walter – with – playing

25C

Setze die *frequency adverbs* an die richtige Stelle.

1. I get tired when I walk the dog. *(never)*
2. Mum goes shopping in the morning. *(usually)*
3. In summer we have barbecue parties in our garden. *(sometimes)*
4. You can ask me for help. *(always)*
5. Joe is there when we need him. *(always)*
6. My grandma has seen the ocean. *(never)*
7. You will see sheep in Scotland. *(often)*
8. Dad and I go fishing on Sunday morning. *(sometimes)*
9. There was milk in the bottle when I wanted to drink some. *(hardly any)*
10. You will hear of Jimmy in the future. *(often)*
11. Dad does the crossword puzzle in the Sunday paper. *(always)*
12. People are afraid when they got to the doctor. *(usually)*

25A–C

Bilde sinnvolle Sätze mit den durcheinander geratenen Satzteilen. Alle „Regeln" sind dabei zu beachten.

1. sometimes – drive – Rita – to – Bob – and – sea – the – in – summer
2. are – livingroom – the – in – news – the – my – watching – parents
3. his – lunch – brings – Jeff – always – to school
4. knows – from – someone – my – dad – town – this
5. we – often – meet – friends – at – the – weekend
6. stands – our – always – in – the – tree – livingroom – Christmas
7. two – books – reads – three – my – or – mum – usually – every – week
8. hear – our – hardly – neighbours – can – come – we – home – ever

The Word Order

DURCHSTARTEN

Deutsch

für die 5. Schulstufe NEU
ISBN 3-7058-6451-3
Dein Übungsbuch 5 NEU
ISBN 3-7058-6454-8
für die 6. Schulstufe NEU
ISBN 3-7058-6452-1
Dein Übungsbuch 6 NEU
ISBN 3-7058-6455-6
für die 7. Schulstufe
ISBN 3-7058-5159-4
für die 8. Schulstufe
ISBN 3-7058-5160-8
für die 9. Schulstufe
ISBN 3-7058-5659-6

Durchstarten mit der neuen Rechtschreibung
ISBN 3-7058-5057-1

Deutsch Rechtschreib-Training
für die 5. Schulstufe
ISBN 3-7058-5399-6
für die 6. Schulstufe
ISBN 3-7058-5524-7
für die 7. Schulstufe
ISBN 3-7058-6004-6
für die 8. Schulstufe
ISBN 3-7058-6261-8

Durchstarten in Deutsch. Grammatik
ISBN 3-7058-6496-3

Englisch

für die 5. Schulstufe NEU
ISBN 3-7058-6456-4
Dein Übungsbuch 5 NEU
ISBN 3-7058-6458-0
für die 6. Schulstufe NEU
ISBN 3-7058-6457-2
Dein Übungsbuch 6 NEU
ISBN 3-7058-6459-9
für die 7. Schulstufe
ISBN 3-7058-5360-0
für die 8. Schulstufe
ISBN 3-7058-5162-4

Englisch
mit Hörverständnis-Training
mit Audio-CD
für die 5. Schulstufe
ISBN 3-7058-5332-5
für die 6. Schulstufe
ISBN 3-7058-5398-8
für die 7. Schulstufe
ISBN 3-7058-5360-0
für die 8. Schulstufe
ISBN 3-7058-5525-5

Mathematik

für die 5. Schulstufe NEU
ISBN 3-7058-6451-3
Dein Übungsbuch 5 NEU
ISBN 3-7058-6463-7
für die 6. Schulstufe NEU
ISBN 3-7058-6461-0
Dein Übungsbuch 6 NEU
ISBN 3-7058-6462-9
für die 7. Schulstufe
ISBN 3-7058-5166-7
für die 8. Schulstufe
ISBN 3-7058-5149-7

NEU!

Französisch

für das 1. Lernjahr
ISBN 3-7058-5167-5
für das 2. Lernjahr
Teil A: Adjektiv, Adverb und Hervorhebung von Satzteilen
ISBN 3-7058-5168-3
für das 2. Lernjahr
Teil B: Verb, Bindungsgefüge und indirekte Rede
ISBN 3-7058-5169-1
für das 3. Lernjahr
ISBN 3-7058-5148-9
für das 4. Lernjahr
ISBN 3-7058-5296-5

Französisch
Grammatik-Training
für alle Lernjahre
ISBN 3-7058-6003-8

> je ca. 160 Seiten mit Lösungsheft durchgehend witzig und farbig illustriert, Paperback

Italienisch

für das 1. Lernjahr
ISBN 3-7058-5421-6
für das 2. Schuljahr
ISBN 3-7058-5578-6
für das 3. Lernjahr
ISBN 3-7058-6142-5

Italienisch
Grammatik-Training
für alle Lernjahre
ISBN 3-7058-6327-4

Latein

für das 1. Lernjahr
ISBN 3-7058-5155-1
für das 2. Lernjahr
ISBN 3-7058-5297-3

Übersetzungstraining für Cäsar, Cicero & Co.
ISBN 3-7058-5333-3
Übersetzungstraining für Ovid, Vergil & Co
ISBN 3-7058-5976-5

Nuntii Latini
ISBN 3-7058-5059-8
Durchstarten mit Nuntii Latini 2
ISBN 3-7058-6570-6

Latein
Grammatik-Training
für alle Lernjahre
ISBN 3-7058-5575-1